AMERICAN LABOR

FROM CONSPIRACY
TO
COLLECTIVE BARGAINING

THE SAILORS' UNION
OF THE PACIFIC

Paul S. Taylor

ARNO & THE NEW YORK TIMES
New York   1971

Reprint Edition 1971 by Arno Press Inc.

Reprinted from a copy in the U.S. Department of Labor Library
LC# 70-156427
ISBN 0-405-02946-2

American Labor: From Conspiracy to Collective Bargaining—Series II
ISBN for complete set: 0-405-02910-1
See last pages for titles.

Manufactured in the United States of America

THE SAILORS' UNION
OF THE PACIFIC

PAUL S. TAYLOR, Ph.D.

Instructor in Economics, University of California

NEW YORK
THE RONALD PRESS COMPANY
1923

PREFACE

The seamen of the world today are for the most part unfree. Men ashore, possessing legal liberty, take for granted the rights of personal freedom which enable them to advance and make more secure their economic and social position. Under the laws of the United States alone, and that completely only since 1915, have sailors been fully accorded the rights of free men. Owing to the economic helplessness of seamen and to the assumed necessities of navigation, the peculiar status of the sailor, bound to his vessel by law under penalty of imprisonment for desertion, remains the same today as it was centuries ago.

When the Coast Seamen's Union was founded in San Francisco less than forty years ago, the American merchant sailor in port was helpless in the hands of the crimps, who debauched him, stripped him of his money, self-respect, and the respect of others, and sent him along with shanghaied landlubbers, drugged or intoxicated, aboard the next outbound ship. At sea, aboard many a deep-water vessel he and his shanghaied shipmates were driven by brutal officers who, if the proper speed and skill were not shown, inflicted corporal punishment in forms and amounts sometimes permitted by, sometimes far in excess of, the provisions of the law.

This book sets forth the history of the organization whose efforts have undoubtedly been chiefly responsible for ending these conditions so far as the United States is concerned. The successes of the Sailors' Union of the Pacific are registered in the Maguire, White, and Seamen's Acts, which have destroyed the power of the crimps and freed all seamen who come under American law. Its leaders are the leaders of the American seamen's movement and its policies have become, by adoption, the policies of the seamen of America and Europe. The principles and methods followed by the sailors in achieving such results, and in steering their organization in sagacious and moderate courses in spite of the opposition not only of the shipowners but of such radical elements as the I. W. W., well merit examination by students of organization and management.

Up to the present time little information on this subject has been accessible to the general public. No comprehensive account has been attempted, and the articles in newspapers and magazines, while increasingly frequent of late years, have been fragmentary. The account given in the chapters which follow is based principally on firsthand sources, in particular on the official records or publications of unions, shipowners' associations, government committees, and other bodies, and on files of the San Francisco newspapers. This information has been checked and supplemented by personal interviews with many of the men personally concerned in the events narrated. The sources chiefly used in connection with each section of the discussion are stated in a note at the opening of each chapter.

In the preparation of the volume, I have received ready and valuable assistance from many quarters: union officials, shipowners and their representatives, sailors of present and earlier days—with some of whom I once lived and worked as an ordinary seaman aboard a coasting vessel—longshoremen, and others. In particular I am indebted to Walter Macarthur, United States Shipping Commissioner in San Francisco; to Andrew Furuseth, President of the International Seamen's Union and

Secretary of the Sailors' Union of the Pacific; to Selim A. Silver, former editor of the *Seamen's Journal*, and A. J. Dickie, editor of the *Pacific Marine Review*, who read my manuscript and gave many helpful criticisms; and to Paul Scharrenberg, editor of the *Seamen's Journal* and Secretary of the California State Federation of Labor.

I desire to express my appreciation of the assistance given by my colleagues in the Department of Economics of the University of California, and especially I desire to acknowledge indebtedness, for stimulating suggestion and helpful guidance throughout the preparation of the work, to Dr. Solomon Blum, inspiring teacher and friend.

For what is said in these pages, however, I assume full responsibility. All possible care has been taken to set forth only what is supported by the best historical evidence. By the free use of quotation I have frequently included evidence in the text.

PAUL S. TAYLOR.

Berkeley, California,
September 1, 1923.

CONTENTS

The Sailors' Union

of the Pacific

CHAPTER I

SEAMEN AND SEAMANSHIP[1]

Serfs and Sailors

In the Middle Ages when men ashore were bound in serfdom to the soil, the seaman was comparatively free. The serfs on the manor were born into bondage; their rights and obligations were prescribed without choice on their part by the customs and laws of the manor on which they were born. But the sailor was a comparatively free agent. While subject to the laws and customs of the sea, he was free to make his own contract with the vessel upon which he chose to embark. The limitations upon his status as a free man extended only through the period of his service aboard ship, during which he sacrificed, to a certain degree, his personal freedom. With the termination of his contract he was again wholly free.

With the passage of time the landsman has become free. Serfdom and human slavery ashore have practically disappeared. But the revolutions and emancipating decrees of Europe, and the thirteenth amendment in the United States, have passed the sailor by. The passage of time has not only failed to remove his bondage to the vessel, but statutory enactment has further stamped his status as peculiar and unfree.

---

[1] Sources for this chapter, in addition to personal investigation and interviews, are:
United States Bureau of Navigation. Annual Reports of the Commissioner of Navigation. Washington, 1884——.
Excerpts from earlier maritime laws:
Pardessus, Jean Marie. Collection de lois maritimes antérieures au XVIIIe siècle. 6 Vols. Paris. 1828–1845.
Twiss, Sir Travers, ed. Monumenta juridica. The Black Book of the Admiralty. 4 Vols. London, 1871–1876.

The Question of Desertion—Medieval Codes

It has been regarded, at least in later medieval and modern times, as a necessity of navigation that peculiar restraints should be imposed upon seamen to compel the performance of their contracts of personal service aboard ship.

The *Consolato del Mare,* compiled in Barcelona, provided:

If any mariner shall run away from his ship or vessel, after he has received his wages in any place, before he has completed the service, which he promised to perform when he engaged himself, that is to say, if he runs away before the ship has made and finished the voyage for which he has engaged himself, and if, further, the mariner above said has sailed on part of the voyage, such mariner is bound to pay back the wages which he has received, to that managing owner of the ship or vessel from whom he has received it, without any dispute; and he ought to have nothing for the services which he has performed, since he has run away in the manner aforesaid: on the contrary, in whatever place he may be sued, he ought to be seized and remain in prison until he has restored to the managing owner of the ship the wages which the said mariner has received, and all the losses and mischiefs that the managing owner has sustained; and the managing owner shall be believed upon his mere word and without witnesses.

The *Judgments of Oleron,* their title derived from a small island off the coast of France, gave the master economic power over the seaman to prevent desertion by holding as follows:

A ship arrives to discharge. The mariners wish to have their wages. And there are some who have neither cot nor chest on board, the master may retain of their wages in order to take the ship back to the place whence he brought it, if they do not give good security to perform the voyage, and this is the judgment in this case.

The *Maritime Laws of Wisbuy,* of triple origin— Baltic, Dutch, and Flemish or Gascon—included the provision just quoted from the *Judgments of Oleron,* and added further the death penalty should desertion actually take place:

If a seaman deserts his ship, and carries away what he has received of the master, and the master apprehends him, the fact being proved upon him by the depositions of two other seamen, he shall be condemned to be hanged, and executed.

These three great medieval codes formed as it were a continuous chain of maritime law, stretching from the easternmost ports of the Baltic Sea, along the Atlantic coast, through the Straits of Gibraltar to the eastern shores of the Mediterranean, and they are the basis upon which modern maritime law rests.

Desertion—Other Early Laws

In addition, various laws of monarchs and of merchants, which likewise form a part of our legal heritage, also limited the freedom of the sailor. The following are examples of these other statutes.

The laws of the Hanseatic League of Baltic and North Sea cities were especially severe. The mildest penalty for desertion embodied in its codes seems to have been imprisonment on a diet of bread and water. In 1380 capital punishment was decreed. This was modified in 1434 and compulsion to serve the voyage substituted. In 1530, however, the death penalty was reimposed. In 1591 it was decreed:

If a sailor or officer who has received one-third wages [customarily paid before sailing] deserts the ship, he shall be branded upon the cheek with an anchor to serve as an example to others.

A similar provision was re-enacted in 1614.

In 1552 Charles V of Spain, because of the difficulties encountered by vessels sailing to America, decreed twenty days' imprisonment for those who broke their contracts to serve aboard ship, and added for good measure, "The sailors . . . . who are not on board to make the entire voyage shall be sentenced to one hundred lashes." In the marine ordinances of 1680, Louis XIV of France decreed:

If a seaman leaves a master without a discharge in writing before the voyage is begun, he may be taken up and imprisoned wherever he can be found, and serve out the time for which he had engaged himself for nothing; and if he leaves the ship after the voyage is begun, he may be punished corporally.

In 1729, in the reign of George II, England passed a statute upon which the United States statute of 1790 seems to have been modeled, providing for the apprehension of deserters, and imposing the penalty of imprisonment in case of refusal to serve. The earliest colonial American law on the subject seems to be a decree of the Colonial General Court of Massachusetts in 1668, providing the penalty of imprisonment in case of desertion.

Desertion—Later Statutes

In 1790 the newly created United States government passed a statute authorizing the arrest of deserting seamen, their detention and return to the vessel. Similar provisions were embodied in the Shipping Commissioner's Act of 1872.

In recognition of the peculiar status of seamen, modern maritime nations have regarded them as "wards of admiralty" incapable of making a freeman's contract, and deserving special care from their guardian, the state. This care has usually taken the form of government hospital service, protection and return of seamen stranded abroad, supervision of the terms of the seaman's contract, of signing on, and paying off under it, and regulation of most of the details of the seaman's relations with the master and the vessel. In fact, with the exception of the rate of wages, the life of the sailor from the moment of signing articles to the time of paying off has always been regulated by law to the minutest detail. Only the power

of self-help and self-protection has been denied. Workmen ashore have long been free to quit work, thereby
incurring the liability of a civil action for damages for
breach of contract, but no criminal liability, for that would
smack of involuntary servitude. On the other hand, the
very word "deserter" applied to the sailor who quits his
ship implies a different status.

Such is the law governing seamen of England, France,
Germany, the Scandinavian countries, and Japan. In fact,
all the great maritime countries of the world apply in
varying degrees the penalty of imprisonment for desertion. Except seamen under the law of the United States
(and that completely only since 1915), except British
seamen in British ports since 1884, except German seamen
who quit before the voyage begins, the legal status of the
sailors of the world today remains unfree. With the
exceptions noted, once they have signed ship's articles,
they are tied to the vessel and can be compelled to carry
out their civil contracts of personal service or become
liable to punishment as criminals for the breach.

The Change from Sail to Steam

The past half-century has witnessed the beginnings of
far-reaching changes affecting the conditions and environ-
ment of those who go down to the sea in ships, changes
which have not yet fully worked themselves out.

On the one hand, it has witnessed the transition from
sail to steam, with one type of marine engine rapidly
superseding another and less efficient type. In the days
when Pacific seamen were organizing, sailing vessels were
still the rule, and steamers the exception. Today, the
proud, white-winged sailers have been nearly superseded
by the less romantic but more efficient steamship. The
report of the Commissioner of Navigation for 1922 gives

the following comparative figures of documented vessels and tonnage of the United States:

Year	SAIL		STEAM	
	Number	Tonnage	Number	Tonnage
1885	18,564	2,771,017	5,399	1,494,917
1922	8,398	2,480,867	18,960	15,982,100

The revolution thus indicated in the means of propulsion has been accompanied by important changes. Seamanship has declined since the days when all sailors served their apprenticeship aboard sailing vessels. The shortening of the time away from port has in no small degree assisted in making possible the improvement of conditions of life and work aboard ship. In the emphasis which will be later laid upon the work and achievements of organized seamen, the background of this underlying change in the mode of ocean transportation must not be forgotten.

World Organization of Seamen

On the other hand, the past half-century has also witnessed a movement of seamen, now organized throughout a large part of the world, for the purpose of ameliorating the conditions surrounding their calling. The contribution of the seamen of the Pacific coast to this movement is the *idea* and its achievement for all seamen touching American ports, of a fundamental change in the legal status of sailors, a change which brings up to the general level of advance a class to which the vestiges of unfreedom still cling. To record and interpret the history of this important branch of the world seamen's movement is the purpose of this book.

It may seem strange that so important a movement first took root on the Pacific coast rather than on the Atlantic which is frequented by more vessels and more seamen of all nations. But these very facts of numbers and variety of races and nations militate against the coming together of seamen in a closely knit organization. The turnover of our seafaring personnel is always high. Boys enter it, remain a few years, and leave for better jobs ashore. When to this difficulty is added that of a rapid and continuous influx and outgo of large numbers of vessels and men of all nations in all trade routes, it will be appreciated that the obstacles to permanent organization were and are greater on the Atlantic coast than on the Pacific.

Conditions Favoring Organization on the Pacific

The underlying conditions which made possible the successful organization of sailors on the Pacific coast are these:

1. The comparative isolation of the Pacific coast (now largely destroyed by the Panama Canal) and the fewness of its ports. As a result, the same group of sailors would be brought together more frequently for social intercourse.

2. The lack of outside competition in the important coastal lumber trade.

This trade is protected against foreign competition by the laws of the United States, which reserve the coastwise trade to American-built vessels of American registry. It is shielded from domestic competition because the lumber schooner is a type of vessel peculiar to the Pacific coast, and the seamen who ship on it must be skilled in stowing lumber as well as in seamanship.

3. A fair degree of racial homogeneity among the coasting seamen of the Pacific.

4. The fact that the offshore trade is of lesser volume than on the Atlantic. There are therefore fewer

numbers to organize, and fewer deep-water sailors available to be used as strike breakers.

5. The high type of sailors attracted to the Pacific coast by the high wages paid there, a fact due largely to the higher wages prevailing ashore.

To these geographical, racial, and economic factors should be added the personal factor of thirty-five years' continuous leadership by a man of compelling personality with a policy big enough to fire the imagination and hold the loyalty of the sailors. In so far as these conditions continue—and it seems likely that most of them will persist—we may expect organization among sailors on the Pacific coast to continue, its backbone in the future as in the past, being the sailors of the lumber schooners.

Make-Up of a Crew—Unions Represented

The crew of a steamer is divided into three departments: deck, engine, and steward's departments. Sailing vessels of course have no engine department, unless they use steam as an auxiliary means of propulsion. Since the movement we are to trace centers about the Sailors' Union of the Pacific, whose members are able seamen, this description of seamen and seamanship will be confined to sailors of the deck department. It is not intended to give the impression at any time that the Sailors' Union is the only organization of seafarers on the Pacific. The masters, mates and pilots, and marine engineers (licensed), cooks and stewards, fishermen, and ferryboatmen (unlicensed) are also organized. The firemen's union even preceded the Coast Seamen's Union by two years. But the Sailors' Union is the recognized leader of the unlicensed personnel. The other Pacific unions have readily co-operated in working for the policies it has mapped out, and it has furnished the principal leadership of the American seamen's movement. For this reason it was selected as the union whose history is most significant to all seamen and most deserving of record in a work which is not comprehensive enough to include detailed histories of all the seamen's organizations on the Pacific.

Duties and Ratings

The supreme command of the ship is vested in the master, or captain, with the first and second mates as subordinates (sometimes also third and fourth mates). The ship's complement consists of these officers, quartermasters, boatswains (quartermasters and boatswains are simply able seamen assigned to particular positions on account of special need or individual skill), carpenters, able seamen, ordinary seamen, and boys. The able seaman, or A.B. (able-bodied), is the standard unit of skill or efficiency on both steam and sailing vessels. He is a man who has had sufficient experience in deck service to acquire the skill in seamanship needed to perform the duties, routine and emergency, required in that service, and who has satisfied the statutory requirements as to experience, knowledge, and skill where laws on the subject exist.

Vessels are of many kinds, and the work on them varies somewhat with the ship, but as a seaman may sail on any type he must be able to perform the duties of his rating wherever he finds himself. In the seventies and eighties at least three years were required for a man to work up from boy to A.B. Often it took considerably longer. The A.B. is supposed to know everything connected with appareling, rigging, and operating a ship. He should be able to cast the lead and give accurate soundings, to hand, reef, and steer in all kinds of weather, to splice hemp or wire rigging, mend sails, clean ship, and use a paint brush for every purpose from applying tallow on the ship's bottom in drydock to putting gilt on her masthead. He should be able to stow and break cargo, to go aloft and use any part of the running rigging in any kind of weather, day or night, and to make all kinds of repairs at sea or in port. He must be able to meet all emergencies, such as fire, stranding, collision, loss of rudder, disabled engines, shifting cargoes, or water-logged ship.

Steam and Seamanship

The introduction of steam has modified the indispensability of practical seamanship on the part of the deck crew in ordinary weather and circumstances. Nevertheless, for the lumber schooners which are so important on the Pacific coast, skill in loading remains important in order that it may be possible both to carry a maximum cargo, and to secure a properly trimmed ship. Skill in loading and discharging is still important in speeding up the "turn around" in port. A good crew can also make repairs aboard ship, which makes it possible to keep the vessel in more continuous operation and saves repair bills. In an emergency, skill and a good pair of sea legs are as essential to the safety of life and property as on a sailing vessel. And a veteran seaman on any ship has the not insignificant advantage of training in the discipline and traditions of the sea.

Ordinary Seamen

An ordinary seaman (O.S.) is one who is learning the trade—a grade below A.B. Under present American law an O.S. does not qualify for the issuance of an able seaman's certificate until after a three years' apprenticeship. However, graduates of school ships conducted under rules prescribed by the Department of Commerce may become able seamen after one year's sea experience and the passing of an examination prescribed by the Department; also seamen of eighteen months' experience who pass the examination prescribed by the Department of Commerce.

Apprentices

An apprentice, or boy, is anyone on his first voyage. He cannot be expected to know anything about the ship. He is to be set to work with old seamen so as to learn a sailor's duties, is to be allowed to steer in fine weather, and to be sent aloft after he has recovered from his first spell of sea-sickness, in order that he may become accustomed to the motion of the vessel and learn to move about the rigging. In recent times it has become very rare to carry apprentices aboard American vessels. Under the Postal Subsidy Act of 1891, mail vessels are required to carry one native apprentice for each 1,000 tons gross register. This requirement is complied with in a perfunctory manner which accomplishes little or nothing toward training American boys in seamanship.

These are the ratings and duties in the deck department of those who go down to the sea in ships. In general, for ships of the same type, they have remained the same from the heyday of the sailing ships down to the present. Comparable ratings have been customary in the vessels of all nations for centuries. The transition from sail to steam, however, is diminishing the number of seamen of the old school whose three or more years before graduation as able seamen were all spent on the deck of a sailing vessel.

Ship's Articles

When sailors engage to serve on vessels, they do so by signing articles. These articles constitute the contract between the vessel and the men who sign. In them are set forth the name of the ship, the prospective voyage, the time of termination of the contract, the rate of wages, and any other agreements which may be inserted to regulate the terms of the special contract. The master signs, and each sailor signs according to his rating and for the wages set opposite his name, whether he be able seaman, ordinary seaman, or boy. For foreign voyages, articles are signed before a United States Shipping Commissioner as prescribed by law. In earlier days in the coastwise trade, and before the Shipping Commissioner's Act (1872) in the foreign trade, articles were signed aboard ship, in the owners' offices, in sailors' boardinghouses, at clothing dealers, on the wharves, or any place where men could be got to sign. When men could not be got in a regular way they were "shanghaied," that is, drugged or intoxicated and forcibly carried aboard regardless of their own will in the matter. In recent times, when the union controlled employment men were shipped through the union office shipping list, or, when that was abolished, on the wharves directly by the masters. Now that the owners are in the saddle (1923), all men employed by them are shipped through their own employment office. The Shipping Board has its own shipping office for sailors who man government-operated vessels.

Wages

The rate of wages is one part of the seaman's contract which maritime law has not sought to regulate. As left to the free play of economic forces and of custom, wages of sailors have varied according to the trade in which the ship was engaged, and according to the wages of the port in which the crew was shipped. Coastwise vessels have usually paid the highest wages, being protected from competition with foreign vessels paying lower wages, and also being forced to compete with the higher rates of wages paid in occupations ashore. Wages on the Pacific coast lumber schooners have customarily varied according as the port of loading is an inside (protected) or outside (open roadstead) port. Before the war, steamers generally paid more than sailing vessels, coastwise vessels more than offshore vessels, and vessels going to outside ports more than those going to inside ports. During the period of the war, at the request of the union, a uniform wage was set for all vessels and runs, but since the breaking of the union power in 1921 the old differentials have reappeared.

The wage figures given in this book usually refer to monthly rates below which union men resolve not to sail. These wages are paid by some owners on some vessels. They may or may not be paid on other vessels belonging to the same or other owners. Where there is an agreement with an association of owners, the union wage of course closely approximates the average wage paid on all vessels sailing on the coast.

CHAPTER II

THE SEAMEN OF THE LATER NINETEENTH CENTURY[1]

The Sailor of the Eighties

The average sailor of the eighties was a good-hearted, carefree fellow, generous to a fault, sound of limb, and, especially on the Pacific coast, an excellent seaman, well trained in his craft. Only a very small percentage had homes and families. A very large and continually increasing proportion was foreign born, attracted to the Pacific coast by the higher wages paid in vessels on that coast. Being thus a migratory class, with few steadying influences, when at sea cut off from society a large part of the time, they easily became, when ashore, a prey to a low class of associates who offered them a "good time" while in port. Thus the "drunken sailor" became a familiar figure on the waterfront and afforded much ground for the judgment that "Jack" was "intemperate, rough, and turbulent in character."

The Modern Sailor

This type of sailor, so frequently held up to public pity and scorn, still may be seen lounging about the waterfront. But, especially among the coasting seamen, there

---

[1] Sources for this chapter, in addition to those mentioned in the text, are:
California Bureau of Labor Statistics,
  Investigation by the Commissioner of the Bureau of Labor Statistics into the Condition of Men Working on the Waterfront and Board of Pacific Coast Vessels, Sacramento, 1887.
Reports of Commissioner of Navigation (see page 3).
Seamen's Journal. (Weekly.) (From 1887 to 1918 entitled *Coast Seamen's Journal.*) San Francisco, 1887——.
Files of following San Francisco newspapers: *Alta California* (1849 ——), *Bulletin* (1855——), *Chronicle* (1865——), and *Examiner* (1865——).

is a considerable and growing group of a more substantial type. These men wear good clothes when they come ashore, have some money in the bank, live in good sailor boardinghouses or uptown, attend the better amusements which the cities afford, and, if met on the street, would not be distinguished from other good citizens who work ashore. Old union sailors say the proportion who are married and have families—among the coasting seamen particularly—is considerably larger than thirty years ago. Married seamen, however, are still much in the minority.

Money and effort have always been freely expended for the moral and spiritual improvement of the seamen. The Commissioner of Navigation in 1885 thought these efforts were "all without much show of success." But whether of any real benefit to the sailor or not, "Jack" himself, although not opposing attempts to provide wholesome recreation, quarters, and companionship while in port, has always been the loudest to protest against what he believed to be misguided efforts, accomplishing nothing for his material well-being as a necessary basis for a higher standard of life.

The Sailor and the Public

The seamen themselves have expressed their complaint of the public ignorance and misconceived attitude toward those of the seafaring class in the following language:

The sailor's life has been, almost from time immemorial, the object of thousands of literary efforts; but those stories of a fantastic type, written in a highly romantic strain, amid the cosy and comfortable surroundings of the author's study, have, if anything, only resulted in rendering still more obscure the true condition of our craft. American boys do not go to sea, as a rule, except they, by reason of family ties, are assured of being in a short time the officers of vessels; and in the short time they do serve as boys they are kept aft. By such means they learn to look upon men in the forecastle somewhat in the same way as the young southerner was trained to look upon the negro. This feeling has communicated itself to the people ashore, and today the sailor is described as a homeless kinless loon, standing outside of the pale of civilization. . . . A prominent citizen will defend low license by saying that there must be low dens on the city front for the accommodations of the sailors. A judge on the bench will warn the jury against the testimony of sailors, reminding them that they are too much addicted to spinning yarns.

Even those who professed to extend a charitable and friendly hand to the seaman became aids to his undoing. Sailors' "homes" were too much like the other sailor boardinghouses. "An Old Salt" has the following to say of the "Seamen's Friend Society":

The Seamen's Friend Society. And who are they? We have heard of them for some three score years or more, but although we have traversed the salt seas for many years in every capacity, from the fo'castle to the cabin, we have never been able to discover what the Seamen's Friend Society has done for "poor Jack."

For many years feeling ran particularly high against the home for seamen maintained by the Ladies' Seamen's Friend Society of San Francisco. The Seamen's Protective Association in 1880 gave vent to the oft-repeated charge that it was

a speculation to make money for some of the members and their friends, that the principal stock in trade for the amelioration of "poor Jack's" condition consisted of Bibles, tracts, a pastor, missionary, and boardinghouse keeper who belonged to a secret society of his class whose interests were diametrically opposed to those of the sailor.

Seven years later, in the first issue of the *Journal* of the new union, the Ladies' Seamen's Friend Society was again bitterly attacked for the same reason, as

a body of women, well meaning, but, ah, so misguided, and knowing nothing for the benefit of your "friends" beyond stuffing their chests with religious books and tracts and providing us with a grave for the sum of $2.50—securing our bodies after death, but leaving us while alive a prey to the landsharks which swarm around us.

There was no help for the seaman from those above him. The files of the San Francisco newspapers are filled with articles and editorials portraying the evil lot of sailors, especially in that port, and urging the public to adopt this or that remedy. But aside from a few successful prosecutions of brutal officers, prosecutions of boardinghouse runners, mostly unsuccessful, and the passage of ineffective laws, the interest, sympathy, and pity of the public brought no permanent benefit to the sailor.

The Sailor Afloat

At sea, the treatment accorded the seaman was such as is scarcely credible to the landsman. Founded on the unequal legal status of seamen and under the guise of discipline as interpreted by the courts, brutal treatment of sailors aboard deep-water ships became flagrant and general.

By the law of 1835, which remained unchanged until 1898, beating, wounding, imprisoning, withholding suitable food, and other punishments inflicted by the master were punishable "if without justifiable cause." Read conversely, this was interpreted to permit such punishment if in the reasonable judgment of the master it was justifiable. The early leading case of *Butler v. McClellan*, 1806, laid down the rule which later courts followed until 1898, when all forms of corporal punishment were declared unjustifiable by the White Act:

The simple and somewhat rude character of seamen . . . renders a prompt and energetic government indispensably necessary to good discipline. . . . There is good sense in the remark of one of the latest and most valuable French writers on maritime law on this subject. "It is impossible to hasten a manoeuvre if the command may not be accompanied with coercive means. Here neither gentleness nor politeness are in place; the punishment of the moment is necessary to quicken the caviller and the lazy." . . . When it is apparent that punishment is merited . . . [the court will not]adjust very accurately the balance

between the magnitude of the fault and the quantum of punishment. It would be holding the master to too severe a rule to
amerce him in damages, because in a case where punishment was
deserved, he may, in the opinion of the court, have somewhat
exceeded the limits of a moderate and reasonable chastisement.

But even had the law been less favorable to the master, it
would have been difficult for the sailor to secure actual
justice. To protect brutal mates, captains used to send
them ashore so that they might escape as soon as the ship
dropped anchor and before the seamen could leave ship
to go before the courts. Later the mates would quietly
return, perhaps under an alias, for the next voyage. Not
until 1898 was it made the legal duty of masters to surrender guilty mates. And if the seamen lodged a complaint against a captain, the latter prepared a bill of exceptions, filed bonds, and sailed away, but the poor seaman,
without money or work, was told to wait two or three
months until the court could hear his case.

Nor was there any remedy against the owners of a
vessel whose captain committed wilful and malicious
assaults on the seamen. As such assaults were regarded
as without the scope of the master's authority, the seaman was without even a legal remedy against the owners
who employed brutal masters. As against the "buckos"
themselves, under the "justifiable cause" law courts and
juries "consistently approved the declaration of accused
persons that assaults upon seamen were justifiable, or, at
any rate, they were deemed such."

Under these conditions life on American deep-water
vessels became well-nigh intolerable, and the number of
native Americans who went to sea grew steadily less. The
abolition of flogging by federal statute in 1850 merely
changed the forms of punishment practiced. The details
of one or two cases are worthy of record here, for no

mere adjectives give an adequate description of conditions aboard an American "floating hell."

American "Hell-Ships"

The ship "Sunrise," Captain Robert K. Clarke, sailed from New York to San Francisco in 1873. The abridged description of the voyage is as follows:

> As soon as the Sunrise got into the stream, the brutalities upon the crew commenced, and did not end until she took a pilot off the Golden Gate. They were knocked down, kicked, beaten with ropes' ends, iron belaying pins, tar buckets, staves, or anything that came handy. But the favorite punishment of the captain and his mate seems to have been the horrible torture known as tricing up, which consists of ironing a man by the wrists, passing a rope around the irons, and hoisting him up until his toes barely touch the deck. They were tortured on the Sunrise in this way for six, eight and ten hours for trivial offenses, or for no offenses at all. . . . Five men seem to have been singled out for special cruelties. . . . These men were maltreated in every possible way—beaten and kicked until they were a mass of bruises and discolored flesh, hung up by the wrists until their hands were black, kept without sleep and set to the hardest and most impossible tasks. One . . . escaped from his torture two days after the vessel left Sandy Hook, by going overboard. A second one . . . followed his example soon afterwards; a third, a boy of about 17, found in the sea a refuge on the morning of the 4th of July—the anniversary of the great declaration of freedom and equality.

Both captain and mate were convicted in this case, largely through the efforts of Henry George and his San Francisco *Post*.

A British writer, Lubbock, in his "Round the Horn Before the Mast," similarly describes the happenings aboard American ships.

> On some of the Yankee hellships the things that go on are almost incredible, and the captains have to be skilled surgeons to cope with the work of destruction wrought by their mates.
> Legs and arms broken were considered nothing, ribs stamped in by heavy sea-boots had to mend as best they could, faces smashed like rotten apples by iron belaying pins had to get well or fear worse treatment, eyes closed up by a brawny mate's fist had to see. There have been many instances of men triced up in

the rigging, stripped, and then literally skinned alive with deck scrapers.

Thus the reputation of American ships has got so bad that none but a real tough citizen, or a stolid long suffering Dutchman (as sailors call all Germans, Swedes, Norwegians, or Russian Finns), will ship in them.

The names of the "Gatherer," "T. F. Oakes," "Commodore T. H. Allen," "Solitaire," and others are still fresh in the minds of old seamen as among the notorious vessels of the eighties and nineties. The San Francisco *Post* of March 14, 1882, tells the story of the "Gatherer."

The ship Gatherer was officered by Captain C. N. Sparks, William Watts, first mate, Cornelius Curtis, second, and John Driscoll, third, all of them comparatively young men. The ship sailed from Antwerp in September last, and scarcely had she touched the deepwater before the fiendish brutality of Watts and Curtis was displayed. Their first amusement was to unmercifully thrash a sailor named Peter Clark for a trifling breach of discipline. Shortly afterwards they beat a man named Turner so badly that he was laid up for months. On the 15th of the month on which the vessel sailed, Curtis, the second mate, so dealt with John Hansen that one of his eyes was nearly put out, and his mouth so badly injured that he can scarcely eat or speak. On the 20th of the same month John Burns was lashed to the rail and Watts broke his nose and disfigured him with brass knuckles. A boy standing by interfered and was struck by the mate on the head. On October 1st Watts lashed a heavy capstan bar to the back of John Burns and compelled him to walk up and down the deck, kicking him as he passed. . . . The next day McCue and George being partially stripped were compelled to have straps fastened around their waists and to draw each other across a certain line. The result was that George, to escape further torture, jumped into the sea and was drowned. It is also stated that a seaman named Hansen was so brutally treated that he jumped overboard and committed suicide. It is charged that the captain did not attempt to save his life. On November 25th the mate struck another sailor with a belaying pin and broke his nose. . . . The mate also struck the steward of the ship over the head, put him in confinement and kept him without food for five days. He was landed at San Pedro a lunatic, and is now confined at Los Angeles. On November 15th McCue being partially stripped was fastened by a strap to his waist and raised up to the mizzen stay and held head downward until he was black in the face from the rush of blood to his head. . . .

These two outstanding instances, which were brought vividly to the attention of the San Francisco public, are representative of innumerable cases of cruelty with which the records of deep-water life are filled. In the coastwise trade, treatment was much better, but on deep-water vessels brutality was the rule, even up to the close of the century.

Defenses for Rough Handling

In defense of the conduct of ship's officers, it was urged that the vigorous use of force was necessary to maintain discipline aboard ship, and to teach the luckless and incompetent shoemakers, clerks, and tailors who awoke from a drunken stupor to find themselves shanghaied aboard ship as able seamen. As explained in the San Francisco *Alta* of November 18, 1866, referring to the common practice of shanghaiing,

. . . consequently, dissatisfied men compose a ship's company, who, by shirking their duty and frequently refusing to obey orders, bring upon themselves some of the punishment that we see so often spoken of as "cruelty to seamen."

In the case of a whaling captain who confessed to charges of cruelty, it was argued that the penalty of the law should not be enforced lest the whaling fleet change its rendezvous to the Hawaiian Islands to the detriment of San Francisco's commerce. These were the defenses of the vigorous use of physical punishment which (except the last) were often echoed approvingly in the press. The seamen, for their part, liable to heavy penalty for assaulting an officer, trained in the sea lore which has always taught implicit obedience, compelled by law to submit to corporal punishment if deemed "for justifiable cause," were individually unable to resist. The result was as has been pictured.

Forecastles

The sailor's quarters aboard ship were in the fore-castle. In the very old ships the forecastle was located between decks. With a small opening onto the deck per-haps 36 inches square, the ventilation was exactly such as might be expected in a narrow-necked bottle. When in stormy weather this opening was covered over, the analogy was complete even to the stopper. In ships built after the Civil War the forecastle was more likely to be above decks, which was a considerable improvement. Most persons are familiar with the descriptions of forecastles in the romantic tales of sea life. Here is a description in 1874 by a surgeon of the United States Marine Hospital Service:

> No prison, certainly none of modern days, so wretched but life within its walls is preferable, on the score of physical com-fort, to the quarters and the life of the sailor on the vast majority of merchant vessels. No gaol dietary so meagre, no penal servi-tude so exacting, no exertion of authority so unrestrained and brutal, no such utter want of care and forethought for health and life of convict or felon, as are the rule, and not the excep-tion, for the man before the mast, would be tolerated, if com-prehended, by the community.

This explains why so many seamen fell victims of con-sumption while engaged in an open-air occupation which one would ordinarily expect to be the most healthful.

In the matter of food American ships usually had a better reputation than foreign vessels. Yet cases of scurvy continued to be frequent in our merchant vessels fourscore years after the remedy was well known and laws had been enacted to compel an adequate and proper dietary including antiscorbutics. In the years 1872–1874, 119 vessels with scurvy aboard were reported by the United States Marine Hospital Service from the Pacific district alone.

Personal Equipment—Then and Now

Today when a man goes to sea, a mess room, dishes and tableware, and bedding are provided, and the sailor takes aboard his canvas bag and perhaps a suitcase with whatever extras he wishes. Vessels in the offshore trade since 1884 have been required to carry slop-chests from which sailors may purchase needed clothing and tobacco with which they may not have supplied themselves before coming aboard, or which may be needed on account of sudden changes of climate or the length of the voyage.

But in former days when a man went to sea he carried most of his equipment with him. A bit of simple mess gear which he kept on a small shelf at one end of his bunk in the forecastle and usually threw away at the end of the voyage, a suit of oil clothes, flannel shirt or guernsey frock, sea boots and a "sou'wester" constituted most of the outlay with which he went on board.

A Life of Discomfort

At best the old-time sailor's lot was a hard one. Sleeping and eating in a little, black, ill-ventilated, poorly lighted, unfurnished hole called a forecastle, with a hard board bunk and a bit of straw or a cheap mattress, if he provided it himself, he lived a life of great physical discomfort. Often working without change in garments soaked with salt spray, or scantily clad, he became a ready victim to rheumatism, and when improperly fed there was the additional menace of scurvy. At the master's disposal 24 hours a day, liable to all kinds of disasters at sea, water-logged ship, fire, famine, shifting cargo, stranding in a gale, loss of vessels sometimes so heavily insured as to be worth more at the bottom of the sea than afloat— these are things of which the landsman has little conception, but they were most real in the life of the sailor at sea.

The Sailor Ashore

At the end of the voyage "Jack" came ashore for diversion that would enable him to forget his troubles. But his pleasures were brief and expensive, for he found himself caught in a perfidious system that quickly stripped him of his money and independence and then again sent him to sea and to another port where the process was repeated. As stated by the California Labor Commissioner, he was "never out of the hands of sharpers, who coax, wheedle, debauch and pander to his worst vices, until his last dollar is gone." The "crimp" (who made his living by furnishing ships with crews) was chiefly responsible for this reception, and his welcome was in this spirit, "All you have to do is to be friendly to 'Jack' and you can empty his pockets and his soul."

The "Crimps"

The crimp, or shipping master, and the boarding master were sometimes two persons, but more usually one and the same. The deep-water boarding masters in the early sixties, and later the coasting boarding masters, organized into associations to control the sailor market. These crimps maintained their hold upon the sailor by controlling his employment. The law allowing holding of sailors' clothing for debt strengthened this power over the sailor, and the payment of wages in advance made the business profitable. And because a sailor in a deep-water vessel was entitled to two, three, or four months' "advance," as it was called, and was especially helpless, the deep-water boarding masters were the first to gain control of their sailor market, and the last to give it up. The coasting boarding masters were never so powerful, nor was their reign so long. But during the decades in which the boarding masters were in control no master could get a crew except from the crimps, and then only after paying them the sailors' advance. Nor could a sailor get a ship except through the same agency.

Control of the market was gained by purchase from captains of the exclusive privilege of shipping men, if men were plentiful. When men were scarce, the captains were forced to pay the crimps for crews. This practice was known as the payment of "blood money" and was so named because drugged or knocked-down men shanghaiied aboard ship were frequently put aboard in an insensible condition, and sometimes covered with blood.

Here is the way in which the system worked as described by the California State Labor Commissioner after an investigation of waterfront conditions in 1887. A ship entering the Golden Gate was met by the first boardinghouse runner who could reach her, even before the vessel dropped anchor. The runner

goes aboard, professes great friendship and sympathy for the sailor, makes glowing promises about work and wages ashore, plies him with whiskey, and finally induces him to leave his ship. The sailor goes ashore, and by so doing generally forfeits wages due him.

Captains of vessels with the prospect of a long stay in port, often take a hand in this, by abusive treatment of their men, in order that they may desert the ship, and thus make a clear gain to the owners of the sailors' accrued wages. This method of doing business is known among seafaring men as "working off." The boardinghouse keeper into whose clutches the sailor falls, keeps him and supplies him with liquor and other unaccustomed luxuries, until his money is gone and a large bill is charged against him.

Then, and not until then, the boardinghouse keeper procures him a berth on board a ship, taking care, however, that the Captain will secure him the payment of all charges against the badly fleeced victim. . . .

Sailors are charged extortionate rates for bringing them off the vessels and taking them on, for discounting their due bills, for commissions on account of getting them berths, and for other services.

Often the process was not so slow as this. Instead of having to sit in a boardinghouse, waiting until his money was gone, deep-water "Jack" was frequently hustled off to sea the very next morning on board the first vessel outward bound. For this short stay the boarding master demanded and received $60 advance of the sailor's wages to pay his indebtedness and to furnish him a cheap outfit with which to go to sea again. Such charges were grossly extortionate.

A cordial understanding seems to exist between the boarding-house keeper and a certain class of sailors' supply dealers. Masters of vessels are not ignorant of the cooperative schemes of which the sailor is the victim, and some even share in the spoils.

The sworn testimony of all proves that it is next to impossible for a sailor to get a berth, or what they term a "chance," without the aid and intervention of a boardinghouse keeper or "master."

The latter goes to the Captain of a coast vessel and by paying a stipulated sum, induces him to agree to ship all his men through the said boarding master's agency.

Notwithstanding that all the boardinghouse keepers who were examined denied that they paid this money, facts have come to the knowledge of the Commissioner, upon personal inquiry, which leave no room to doubt its being done.

"Advance"

The crimps thus took all the wages earned by the sea-men on the incoming voyage, and by means of the advance or allotment note, mortgaged most of his outbound wages. If the seaman protested his indebtedness, or objected to shipping as the boarding master ordered him, his clothes were held by the boarding master for debt. This was a very effective club held over his head, for without money or clothes the sailor could not get very far. The laws allowing advance or allotment to an "original creditor," and holding of clothing for debt were the cornerstones upon which the nefarious system rested.

It all meant virtual economic slavery for the sailor, and perpetual poverty, as he was usually working to pay off a "debt." His wages were seldom his own. And the premium was on the most reckless, improvident spender and heaviest drinker, for the sooner his money was gone, the sooner he got a ship. But the man who tried to be thrifty and save his money had to sit in a boardinghouse just so much longer; not until his money was all gone would the boarding master get him a ship.

Blood Money

Blood money also came out of the sailor, though not so directly. When men were scarce, instead of raising wages, blood money was increased, and more landlubbers were shanghaied aboard by foul means when drugged or intoxicated. More unfortunate landlubbers aboard meant more work for the real seamen, and more driving and brutality by the masters and the mates. Increased blood money meant less wages, so whichever way matters went it was always at the expense of the sailor.

Shanghaiing

This shanghaiing of unwilling, drugged, or intoxicated landsmen to serve in place of able seamen was attended by grave dangers to navigation as well as misfortune and harsh treatment to the crews. In 1884 the United States Consul at Hull, England, complained in a letter to the Commissioner of Navigation:

The wheat ships arriving at this and other ports from San Francisco are manned by the most worthless set of men. Of the large ships here during the past four months, viz., the Reaper, Amy Turner, Solitaire, and Tam O'Shanter, the first named had but two, the second three, the third three, and the last, three men who could be trusted at the wheel to steer. These men were paid from $20 to as high as $40 per month, and, in addition to this, a bonus or "blood-money" is called for by the boarding master to the extent of $15, and as high as $25 for each man. It is little short of a miracle that vessels so manned should safely reach their destination. The large majority of these men are green landsmen, and, as a matter of course, being but of little use on board the ship, they do not receive the best of treatment, and on reaching port desert and become chargeable on some of the consulates. Three months advance pay is demanded at San Francisco, and this, as does everything else, goes to the boarding master. The men are put on board without clothing, and, according to many of them, in a state of intoxication, and without their own consent. Upon arrival here they are in debt to the ships, and, aided by the crimps, and not opposed by the officers, they desert.

Unsuccessful Remedial Attempts

In 1879 a number of San Francisco shipowners passed a resolution against paying blood money. This protest, like others, was entirely ineffective, and the practice continued to thrive. Whenever the owners sought to defy their control, which was seldom, the crimps simply refused to allow a man on board a vessel until their terms had been complied with. When boardinghouse runners were arrested for violation of the law, masters of vessels have felt compelled to intervene and ask dismissal of suits "to save themselves from any appearance of fighting the sailor-running nuisance." A state of affairs which prevailed in ports of the Pacific coast for nearly half a century was described during its heyday, by the San Francisco *Bulletin* as follows:

It is extremely difficult to procure convictions for the offences committed by these runners, as they not only swear each other clear, but oftentimes so manipulate the officers of ships, by the use of money or by threats, that they will not prosecute. . . . The commerce of the port is at their mercy. A crew cannot be shipped without their consent, and ships are frequently compelled to lay in the stream for days and weeks without crews on account of the captain's having in some manner incurred the displeasure of these pests.

The Shipping Commissioner's Act of 1872 struck at shanghaiing by requiring that only sober men could sign

articles before a commissioner.   The boarding masters
fought the act by delaying the ships, and refusing to
furnish crews. They stopped this procedure, however,
when they found that the law could be evaded by having
bright-appearing, sober seamen sign the articles, using as
many different names as desired. They could still shanghai
men, who when they came to their senses aboard ship
found that the "register man" had signed a name for
each of them.

Act of 1884

In 1884 another attempt was made to break the power
of the crimps. The legislators again took a hand in
checking the evil which the Shipping Commissioner's Act
had failed to curb, and which owners and public were
seemingly helpless to prevent. The Dingley Act of June
26, 1884, was passed, which struck at the roots of the
system upon which crimping flourished.

The most far-reaching provision of the act was the
abolition of advance wages, and the prohibition of allotments to anyone except the sailor's wife, mother, or other
relatives. This blow aimed at the vitals of the crimping
system, for if the future earnings of the seamen could
not be mortgaged as a condition of securing employment
there was little money in the business for the boarding
masters, clothiers, and crimps who preyed upon the sailor.
Realizing this fact they used all their power to obstruct
the shipment of crews without advance, thus placing a
great handicap on shipping. As stated by the Commissioner of Navigation in his annual report for 1890:

For two years scarcely a seaman could be shipped except in
violation of the law prohibiting advances. After the passage of
the Act of 1884 many American ships were detained for weeks
and in the end had to settle at the ship's cost the debts of the
seamen to their boarding masters before obtaining crews.

In San Francisco as well as elsewhere the law was frequently evaded by hiring the sailor at $10 a month, paying the rest of the wages due him in the form of a cash bonus to be turned over to the boarding masters. Or if the ship was going to a foreign port where the American law was not rigidly enforced, the boarding master was given a note payable after the ship reached its destination and the wages had been earned.

Between the tying up of ships by the crimps on one hand and wholesale evasion of the law, also forced upon the owners by the crimps, on the other hand, no one was satisfied. As a result, shipowners and crimps united to change the law, and the act of June 19, 1886, was passed, authorizing payment of allotment not exceeding $10 for each month of the contemplated voyage to an "original creditor for any just debt for board or clothing." This was in effect a re-establishment of the advance system for the benefit of the crimps. The $10 a month provision merely put some limits on the spoliation of seamen. And it was evaded in the case of crews signing before foreign consuls, as the previous law had been evaded, by shipping men at a nominal rate, say 25 cents a month, and turning the remainder of what they should really have had over to the crimps. So the sailor was not in much better position than before the effort to prohibit advance.

Desertion in San Francisco

In 1891 a committee appointed by the San Francisco Chamber of Commerce to investigate blood money, after finding that $120,000 at $40 per head had been paid as blood money for one year in San Francisco, made the following report:

Your Committee is of the opinion that this pernicious system has to some extent been encouraged by shipowners themselves, and in this connection reference is made to foreign shipowners, as the crews of American vessels are paid off here, inasmuch as they have not sufficiently endeavored to retain their men on arrival at this port, and have acted, there is reason to believe, from the short-sighted point of view that the unpaid wages of the outward voyage sacrificed by deserters, and the saving of their expenses of maintenance while in port, would compensate for having to ship substitutes in San Francisco at a higher rate of wages. This policy did not contemplate the payment of blood money, but it facilitated the business of crimps and boarding masters, and has doubtless assisted in building up the present pernicious system.

As late as 1903 this working off and desertion of foreign seamen in San Francisco, especially the British, was notorious. Sometimes an average of one-third of the crews deserted during the course of a year. In fact, it was of considerable material importance to the shipowners on the coast, as is evident from a letter of the Secretary of the Shipowners' Association:

> Were it not for the fact that so many of the seamen coming to this port in foreign vessels elect to leave their vessels to take advantage of the higher rates of wages paid on American craft, the shipowners on this coast would find it almost impossible to man their ships. . . .

The crimps, as also the brutality aboard ship, were worse in deep-water shipping, although the coastwise trade was infested until after a long fight by the union, which finally resulted in the enactment of remedial legislation.

Organization a Final Way Out

Fleeced at every turn ashore, kept in continual poverty by those who grew rich through mortgaging his wages, without a home because of his roving occupation and because too poor to support a family, driven by his officers at sea and tied to his vessel, pitied or sneered at by people ashore, the seaman found no effective help from the government which proclaimed itself his guardian, nor material advantage from the aid of those who came to save him, but whose concern was rather the hereafter of his soul than his physical needs of the present. Editorial after editorial in the press made known his plight to the public; and Commissioners of Navigation and Labor reported it to Congress and legislatures, all without permanent effect; laws passed in his behalf were evaded or repealed; ship-owners were indifferent or helpless; masters of vessels were likewise either indifferent or helpless, and not infrequently shared in the profits derived from plunder of the seaman; unorganized, the sailors were powerless. No one knew the degraded condition of the sailor better than himself. No one could lift him out of it but himself, and that only by organization and persistent, self-reliant struggle against great odds. So organize he did.

CHAPTER III

FIRST ATTEMPTS TO ORGANIZE[1]

Early Trade on the Pacific Coast

Sea transportation in and out of San Francisco before the gold rush was not very extensive. The whaling fleet first wintered in San Francisco Bay in 1822, but later, port restrictions were adopted by the Mexican government which drove the whalers to winter in the Sandwich Islands. In 1855 a bill was passed by the California legislature reducing pilotage fees to meet those in the Islands, an action which in the course of time brought back the fleet, as San Francisco Bay was much more convenient.

In 1835 tallow, hides, and grain were the chief articles carried by sea. For many years previous the Russians from the north had visited the Bay annually for meat and grain. American vessels from eastern ports were active in the Pacific coastwise trade, as well as in the whaling industry and Asiatic trade, in which they had participated since before 1800. It was on one of the Yankee vessels of the thirties engaged in the California "drogher" or hide-carrying trade that Dana spent his two years before the mast. English vessels, as well as ships of other European nations, came to share in the

---

[1] Sources of this chapter are:
  Files of San Francisco newspapers (see page 16).
  Books on early history of California.
  Seamen's Protective Association of San Francisco, Minutes, 1880–1882. (Not open to public inspection. Access granted to writer during preparation of this work. Also personal interview with Vice-President John P. Devereux.)
  Cross, Ira B., "First Coast Seamen's Unions," in *Seamen's Journal,* July 8, 1908.

trade with the coast. Spanish ships, however, were conspicuous by their absence except in the trans-Pacific trade between Mexico and Manila prior to 1815. By 1847 a scanty inland commerce had developed, and about a dozen vessels were engaged in the coastwise trade. For the year ending March 30, 1848, 86 arrivals from sea were reported. The population of San Francisco at about this time (August, 1847) was 459.

Fugitive Seamen Laws

Even in these early days the offense of desertion was by no means unknown. In September, 1847, a town ordinance was passed providing a penalty of six months in jail for desertion. It is interesting to record that under this law Lieutenant Gilbert, later the first congressman from the state, upon one occasion scoured the neighborhood with militia and brought back seven deserters. Some years later a state law against desertion was enacted. At least as early as 1846 some persons made it their business to catch runaway sailors at so much a head. Soon the crimps, too, appeared, for by 1855 we find efforts to enact measures against "that disreputable class of persons who made a business of enticing seamen to desert."

The Rush for the Gold Fields

In 1848 the Pacific Mail Steamship Company was organized to carry mail for the government, and three ships, the "California," "Oregon," and "Panama," were built. The "California" sailed from New York late in 1848 before the discovery of gold became generally known. But the news quickly spread, and when she stopped at Panama and other coast ports, she was besieged with people who sought passage to the new gold fields. On the 29th of February, 1849, she arrived at San Francisco. Immediately the entire ship's company, except the commander, purser, and possibly one or two other officers, deserted and left for the mines. It was some time before a crew could be mustered for the return trip, and when they were obtained the seamen demanded and received $200 a month. The "Oregon" arrived a short time after. Her captain, profiting from the experience of the "California," anchored under the protecting guns of the battleship "Ohio," and departed for the the mines, leaving his crew virtual prisoners until he was ready to return to sea again. Notwithstanding, several of the crew managed to escape and joined the rush for gold.

The First Sailors' Strike

Most of the vessels which arrived during the first year after the discovery of gold were left lying at anchor without a soul on board, the crews having left for the mines. In July, 1850, about 500 abandoned ships were lying in the harbor, some of which had not even discharged their cargoes. The wages on the few ships which did continue in operation were enormous. Many of the old ships were sold for port dues, many were dragged ashore and used for stores and lodgings, one was used for a municipal jail, and many sank and rotted at their anchors. The return of the disappointed miners toward the end of 1850 gave many vessels an opportunity to leave port. With the great influx of men desiring passage east wages sank to $25 a month. The sailors struck in August, but there were too many men eager to take their places, so the strike was a failure.

The Days of Windjammers

Most of the vessels at this time were sailing ships. In 1847 the first steam craft appeared in the Bay, a small sidewheeler named the "Sitka," brought down from Alaska. Until 1850, the sailing vessels were of the square-rigged type, but in that year appeared the famous California clipper ships which reduced the sailing time to New York by a month.

The first part of the decade of 1850–1860 was a period of considerable activity in the formation of labor unions, but no organization appeared among the seamen except for the futile strike already mentioned. For a time shipping was brisk, wages were high again, and shanghaiing became common. But after 1853, with the decline of immigration and placer mining, shipping decreased for several years. Deep-water wages dropped to $20 a month, with $40 advance for the boarding master. They remained at this figure for a number of years.

First Sailors' Union of the Pacific

In the period of prosperity immediately following the Civil War a wave of unionism swept over the waterfront. The calkers, ship and steamboat joiners, shipwrights, riggers and stevedores, and steamship firemen were organized. In January, 1866, this notice appeared in the papers:

SEAMEN'S FRIENDLY UNION SOCIETY

All seamen are respectfully invited to attend at the Turn Verein Hall on Bush Street, between Stockton and Powell Streets, on Thursday evening, January 11th, at 7½ o'clock, to form a Seaman's Society for the Pacific Coast.

At this meeting a union was organized and named the Seamen's Friendly Union and Protective Society. Alfred Enquist was elected president, and George McAlpine, secretary. Meetings were held for some months but the membership never became large. The society was unable to pay a salary to its officers sufficient to keep them ashore so that they might care for the interests of the union. The officers were therefore obliged to go to sea, leaving the union rapidly to disintegrate and finally disappear without anything being accomplished.

In the latter part of the same year a strike occurred against an attempted reduction of wages. Coasting vessels which had been paying $40 a month now attempted to lower wages to $30 or $35, as had been usual in preceding years when harvesting ashore was over. Deepwater rates which had been $30 a month and $60 advance since 1862 or 1863 were now lowered to $20 a month and $40 advance. The boarding masters, who wanted the $60 advance, adopted a resolution against the reduction, and instigated the sailors, who were under their power, to resist. Of course it made little material difference to the sailor what wages were, for wages soon came into the hands of the boarding masters anyway. But they united with the boarding masters in opposing the reduction, and several hundred sailors marched through the streets in public demonstration. The strike lasted about three weeks and apparently was sufficient to keep up wages on the coast. A year later coasting wages were still $40 a month, and were paid in gold. But deepwater wages had sunk to $25, and were paid in greenbacks worth 72 cents on the dollar.

Clothing Dealers and Crimps Organize the Sailors

More than a decade elapsed before another effort was made to organize the seamen, this time during a period of general unemployment and discontent, anti-Chinese agitation, and business uncertainty. On the night of

January 31, 1878, a large number of seamen met in the Western House, on Steuart Street, for the purpose of forming a protective association. J. F. Harrison, a clothing dealer, called the meeting to order, and after a short speech reviewing the condition of the sailor, introduced Colonel Heath, J. J. Merritt, and others who addressed the assembly. A union was organized with about 100 charter members, George Ball and O. Svenkeson were elected temporary president and secretary, respectively, and a committee was appointed to draft a constitution and by-laws. At a meeting early in February the boarding-house keepers were asked to join the organization, the purpose of which was to protect the coast seamen from the encroachments of the deep-water sailors who were alleged to be the cause of bringing wages below the level of subsistence.

The Coasting Trade the Origin of Unionism

It is worth noting that this organization, like other organizations of sailors on this coast, began among coasting seamen rather than among deep-water seamen; and this in spite of the fact that the wages of deep-water men were lower, and their conditions much worse than those of the coast sailors. After establishing themselves, these organizations expanded to include deep-water men. The explanation lies in the fact that the coasting sailors were in the same ports oftener, had a wider and closer acquaintance among their fellow seamen, and were a more homogeneous group.

On February 7 the constitution and by-laws were adopted. George Ball and J. F. Harrison addressed the meeting, and Fred Clarke, a boardinghouse master, submitted a resolution that no seaman should ship on a vessel with a Chinese cook or steward. This met with hearty applause, but since Clarke was not a member, the resolution was not voted upon. A similar resolution, however, was adopted some three weeks later. Permanent officers were chosen as follows: J. F. Harrison, a clothing dealer, president, John Lamb, vice-president, George Ball, secretary, James Smith, treasurer, and T. Curtin, a boarding master, sergeant-at-arms. On March 7, Charles Matson, Joseph Louis, and Charles O'Brien were chosen trustees.

By April 2, 1878, the Seamen's Protective Union, as it was named, numbered about 600 members. But shipping, as well as other business, was dull, and enthusiasm waned. The union resolved that its members should not work for less than $30 a month in coasting vessels nor work with Chinese, and forwarded a petition to the legislature requesting that no more public money be spent on the Sailors' Home "with the pretended assertion that we are to be benefited thereby." But it is not known that the Seamen's Protective Union accomplished anything for the good of the sailors, as might have been expected from an organization including boarding masters and clothing dealers. After a few months it disappeared, as had its predecessor.

Seamen's Protective Association

In the latter part of the summer of 1880, the Pacific Mail Steamship Company discharged a number of white employees and put Chinese in their places. A committee of sailors protested, but the company refused to change its position. A meeting of steamship sailors and firemen was then called to meet in Irish-American Hall on August 31, 1880. This meeting was addressed by S.

Robert Wilson, Dennis Kearney, the anti-Chinese agi-
tator, Frank Roney, of the Iron Moulders' Union, Tom
Haggerty, and others.   It was decided to hold another
meeting of those interested in forming a protective union.
Accordingly, at 10 A. M. Sunday, September 5, in Charter
Oak Hall, a group of steamship firemen and sailors gathered to perfect their organization.   Frank Roney was
temporary chairman, and permanent officers were elected
as follows: Frank Roney, president; S. Robert Wilson,
recording secretary; A. J. Starkweather, financial secretary; John Pygeorge, treasurer, and John P. Devereux,
Ernest Lea, and Smith, vice-presidents.   Twenty-seven
men joined.   Roney, a landsman, was elected president instead of a sailor, in order to provide for continuity of
leadership.   Because of the character of his occupation no
sailor could be present at meetings regularly.   Nor was
there any money with which to pay a sailor to remain
ashore in order to look after union affairs.

The new union, which called itself the Seamen's Protective Association of San Francisco, found that it had a
difficult road to travel.   A series of seven mass meetings
through September and early October brought in only
27 new members.   There was continual opposition from
the boarding masters.   The secretary recorded of the
open-air meeting on October 1 that:

during the proceedings there were continuous interruptions by the
boardinghouse land sharks and their whiskey-bought runners;
going even so far as to throw valuable eggs,—that did not have
time to get the proper age and odor—at the agitators, but they
made a bad failure, as the superior intelligence and calmness of
the speakers entirely discomfited their enemies.

Up to December 1 only 113 men had joined, Devereux
having brought most of them by visiting the men on
vessels in port.

Union Activities

But though small in numbers the union concerned itself with whatever problems faced the sailor. Its record is not one of achievement, but it is of value in showing the scope of the protests of seamen against the injustices surrounding them.

The union endeavored to give aid to all seamen, regardless of union affiliation, in bringing to justice ship's officers guilty of the commission of brutalities. But in spite of great efforts and attacks on the United States attorney for laxity in conducting prosecutions, the committee on prosecutions had to report on January 16, 1881, that of the 100 cases of cruelty coming under their notice, no convictions had been secured, with the exception of a fine of $25 in the case of the mate of the "Western Belle." Shanghaiers were prosecuted with somewhat better success. The union protested against the issuance of meal checks by shipowners, asserting the sailor's right to be paid a cash allowance and to eat where he chose. The union appointed a committee to investigate the sailor boardinghouses and report on the quality of food, cleanliness, etc.

First Legislative Efforts

Following upon the news of a shipwreck in which the Chinese seamen became panic-stricken, while the white sailors displayed coolness, good judgment, and skill in handling the situation, resolutions were adopted condemning Chinese seamen as untrustworthy. Frank Roney drafted a bill requiring that two-thirds of the seamen on every ship be citizens of the United States. Efforts were made over a considerable period of time to have the bill introduced and passed by Congress. General Rosecrans, then in Congress, stated his willingness to aid the seamen, but nothing came of the bill. The Ladies' Seamen's Friend Society was the object of bitter and sarcastic attacks in meeting, for its conduct of the Sailors' Home, and for alleged indifference to the real welfare of the seamen. It was also agitated in meeting that Congress be requested to make twelve hours a day's work at sea with double pay for overtime. In those days a request for a twelve-hour day at sea was a limitation of hours.

The Seamen's Protective Association sent delegates to the Trades Assembly in San Francisco, and carried on considerable correspondence with the Australian and the Chicago Seamen's Union. Official affiliation with these two unions was never attained, but members of the Australian union, on at least one occasion, were admitted to the Seamen's Protective Association without payment of initiation fee. In the fall of 1881 the association was made benevolent, providing a payment of $7 a week during the first six months of a member's sickness. Initiation fees were raised to bring in revenue, but it is doubtful if benefits were ever paid to any considerable extent.

Disintegration of the Seamen's Protective Association

The union never attained a large membership. One year after its foundation its roll showed a total joined of 341, of whom only 99 were paid up in full, and 176 had been dropped from the roll as being more than six months in arrears. In the autumn of 1881 interest in the society began to lag. Meetings were held only twice a month instead of weekly, and yet attendance was poor. Between February 3, 1882, and July 18 of the same year no meetings were held. The union met on July 18 only to quarrel. The old trustees charged Frank Roney and

McAvoy with "disobeying and refusing to recognize" their authority in connection with certain financial matters. The trustees accordingly expelled them. On July 25 new officers were elected: William Higgens, president; John P. Devereux, vice-president; Ernest Lea, recording secretary; O'Brien, financial secretary; J. Judge, treasurer. But the new régime was not very active. Efforts to increase the attendance failed. One meeting was held on August 22 and another on October 14. It was found that the treasurer of the organization had taken its funds for his own private use. Devereux, who was now the active leader, prosecuted Judge on behalf of the association. The last meeting of the union was presided over by Devereux on November 4, 1882. No further effort was made to revive the organization.

CHAPTER IV

SUCCESSFUL ORGANIZATION[1]

The Coast Seamen's Union

Through the winter of 1884 and spring of 1885 shipping was dull and wages were low. A wave of unionism was sweeping the country at the time and reached the San Francisco waterfront. The longshore lumbermen, wharfbuilders, riggers and stevedores, steamship joiners, marine firemen, and steamship cooks and waiters were organized; but after three failures the sailors were still unorganized. At this time, however, a spontaneous uprising among the seamen themselves, spurred on, and for a time led, by a group of socialist agitators, was to accomplish the hitherto impossible.

The condition of the sailor was getting no better. He was as much as ever the victim of the boarding masters, crimps, and clothing dealers who preyed upon him ashore. Brutal treatment at the hands of his officers was common and flagrant aboard deep-water ships. Early in March, 1885, came what proved to be the last straw. On the 4th of March news of a further reduction of wages was received. Wages in coasting sailing vessels were to be $25 for open or outside ports, and $20 for others. All that day and the next the seamen gathered in excited groups

---

[1] Sources for this chapter are:
  Coast Seamen's Union of the Pacific coast.
    Constitution and History, 1885.
    Minutes, including records of meetings, reports of officers and committees, and various letters to the union, or written by officers of the union on official business, 1885-1891. (Not open to public inspection. Access granted to the writer during the preparation of this work.)
  Files of San Francisco newspapers (see page 16).
  For the account of the Steamship Sailors' Protective Union, the author is indebted to Daniel Dunn and Nicholas Jortall, former secretaries of the organization.

along the waterfront. Now and again they rallied in larger groups abreast of some vessel that had shipped men at the reduced rates, and persuaded or compelled the crew to leave.

Founding a Union

The seamen's own story of the founding of their union is as follows. The account begins with the 5th of March:

At about noon Sigismund Danielwicz, a member of the International Workmen's Association, who had but lately returned from the Sandwich Islands, where he had been vigorously engaged in the labor struggle, chanced to pass by and inquired the cause of the excitement. He was told, and advised them to form a protective union and join hands with all other labor organizations of San Francisco. This they agreed to do. Mr. Danielwicz engaged to procure the help necessary to organize and the seamen agreed to have the men at a meeting to be held the next night on Folsom Street Wharf.

The next night accordingly, a tumultuous crowd of some three or four hundred coasting sailors gathered under the canopy of the stars alone, on the Folsom Street Wharf around the piles of lumber lying there. The night was pitch dark and the faces of the speakers could not be seen. Mr. Danielwicz had procured them, however, from the organizing headquarters of the International Workmen's Association and the organizer in charge called for nominations for a chairman. Mr. Geo. Thompson was pushed forward and ascended one of the lumber piles. B. B. Carter and Joseph Kelly, of the Steamshipmen's Protective Union [should read "Steamshipmen's Protective Association"], P. Ross Martin, of the Sacramento Knights of Labor, and J. J. Martin, M. Schneider, Sigismund Danielwicz, and Burnette G. Haskell, of the International, all addressed the assemblage and urged them to organize at once. Lists were hastily prepared and opened and some two hundred members signed the roll. Most of them, however, were without money to pay an entrance fee and so the amount collected was comparatively small [222 names and $34.60]. Enough, however, was collected to justify the hiring of a hall for the next night and for doing necessary printing. At twelve P. M. the tired committee had adjourned the meeting until the following night.

Early Union Policies

At the meeting of March 7, held in Irish-American Hall, it was determined "that no owner, captain, boarding-

house keeper or professional politician be ever allowed to
attend or join the union." One hundred and two names
were added to the roll. A committee of 42 members was
appointed to visit the vessels and sailor boardinghouses
for the purpose of getting new members and of keeping
wages up to the rate of $35 for open or outside ports, and
$30 for others. At a meeting on March 9, 132 more
joined, making a total of 456 members. On motion of
Haskell it was resolved to boycott boardinghouses and
shipping offices shipping non-union men. A constitution
and by-laws read by Haskell were adopted with some
amendment, and a suggestion to establish a union shipping
office met with hearty approval. On March 11 permanent
officers were elected: George Thompson, president; Ed
Andersen, J. D. Murray, Michael Sweeney, John Fitz-
patrick, and J. D. Thorner, vice-presidents; Rasmus Niel-
son, secretary; and as Advisory Committee from the International, P. Ross Martin, B. G. Haskell, Martin Schneider,
S. Danielwicz, and James J. Martin. Headquarters were
established at Room 69, 6 Eddy Street, and the waterfront was divided into six sections to be patrolled under
the leadership of the officers in the interest of keeping
wages up and preventing non-union sailors from going to
sea.

The strike which had resulted in the formation of the
union was actively prosecuted. After a short, sharp conflict the owners conceded the wages asked by the men.
But the end of the strike by no means brought peace. The
sailors carried on with great vigor a campaign to increase
their membership and reduce the number of non-union
men shipping from San Francisco. Clashes with boardinghouse masters, captains, and police were common
occurrences on the waterfront whenever a vessel shipped

or tried to ship a non-union crew. This phase of the struggle lasted until the middle of May.

Successes and Failures

The new union grew rapidly. On July 1, 1885, it claimed 2,200 of the 3,000 or 3,500 coasting sailors. Colored sailors were permitted to join at this time, and deep-water seamen. But the latter rarely joined. They had little contact with the coast seamen except when the boarding masters shipped them on coasting vessels to take the places of the coast seamen on strike. A union shipping office was opened at 7 Spear Street with Ed•Crangle as shipping master, and a co-operative union boardinghouse was started at 217 Broadway. The services of the officers and those who ran the boardinghouse were given without pay, but both shipping office and boardinghouse proved to be premature. The union was unable to maintain even a semblance of control of the shipment of sailors against the captains, owners, and Coasting Boarding Masters' Association. Since men had to live in an outside boardinghouse in order to get a ship, the union house made a poor offering to the individual seaman. Throughout the summer the union made occasional raids on the waterfront to prevent "scab" shipping, and in early September the guerrilla warfare was resumed with vigor. But its efforts were unavailing, and the boardinghouse and shipping office had to be given up.

On June 2, 1885, the first step was taken to extend the organization into the various ports of the coast, by the appointment of an agent for San Pedro. It is distinctive of the seamen at this time that they established the branches not as independent locals, but as subsidiaries operating under the same constitution, and as a part of the same union. After July 1, 1885, it was decided to

elect no more presidents. Until January 8, 1886, a vice-
president, or chairman, presided, the last of whom was
Alfred Fuhrman, long active as a leader of the brewery
workers, and now an attorney in San Francisco. From
1886 until after the internal conflict of 1921 it was the
custom to choose a chairman at each meeting of the union.
A voluntary shipwreck fund with a $30 benefit to ship-
wrecked members was maintained from the beginning.

Socialist Influence and Its Decline

The members of the Socialist International Advisory
Committee were active throughout the early years of the
organization. Their influence for the good of the union,
particularly that of Haskell and later Von Hoffmeyer,
cannot be overestimated. Yet at times they led the union
astray. Haskell tried to establish a co-operative land
colony in Tulare County, called "Kaweah Colony." He
secured the backing of many members of the union and
even the investment of some of the union funds on the
argument that it "would give employment for a good
many seamen who would otherwise be idle during the
winter." But though the experiment lasted for several
years it was never a success, and the union failed to receive the great benefits promised. Haskell also tried at
one time to establish a Legion of Honor of those men
within the union who were most prominent; at another
he sought to have a red card issued to the leaders as a
badge of distinction. Both disruptive movements were
promptly checked by the union. Von Hoffmeyer, as a
member of the Socialist International Advisory Committee (he was also a member of the Musicians' Union),
ably represented the seamen's union in the waterfront
investigation of 1887 conducted by the California Labor
Commissioner. He also put the bookkeeping of the union

on a business basis. But with the bitter economic struggle which absorbed the attention of the union during these years, and the rise of strong non-socialist leaders within the union, the influence of the socialists rapidly waned. In 1887 the rule that members of the Advisory Committee must be chosen from the Socialist International was dropped, and two years later the committee was abolished altogether.

The "Bread and Butter" Question

To return to the fights of the coast seamen over what their preamble termed the "one important question, the 'bread and butter question,'" we find 1886 to be a stormy year. On March 4 the union demanded $35 a month on vessels to Puget Sound and all inside ports, $40 to outside ports, and $30 to Mexico, Honolulu, and the South Sea Islands. These wages were successfully maintained. So many deep-water sailors deserted and joined the union to ship on the coast at the advanced rate that the union was obliged to rule that they must present a discharge and pay the high initiation fee of $10, coast seamen paying only $5. Even at the established scale of wages men were scarce, and throughout May shanghaiing was a frequent spectacle on the waterfront.

The Shipowners Organize

On June 3 occurred an event which proved to be most disastrous for the seamen, although they themselves were not the authors of the trouble. The Firemen's Union ordered its men out of the Oceanic Steamship Company's vessels after a dispute over the number of firemen a certain ship should carry. The Federated Trades were appealed to, with the result that a general strike on the vessels of the Oceanic Steamship Company was ordered.

The coast seamen obeyed, those who quit forfeiting their wages in accord with the provisions of maritime law. But a result more disastrous for the seamen than the loss of their wages was the formation on June 7 of the Shipowners' Association of the Pacific Coast. This organization established a shipping office and a continuous discharge or industrial passport system known as "grade books." Masters then refused to sign men unless they had the grade books and shipped through the office of the association. This, of course, was a blow at the Coast Seamen's Union, and amounted to locking the members out unless they would renounce membership in the union. They were, in fact, compelled to surrender their union cards in order to obtain the grade books. This was generally done by the men in order to obtain employment, whereupon the union adopted the policy of issuing duplicate union cards. Non-union men were gathered up from wherever they could be obtained, including deep-water seamen, deserters, or men who had never been to sea before. In the latter part of June blood money rose to $40. The original strike on the Oceanic vessels had affected about 100 sailors, but now the Shipowners' Association was fighting the entire union. These conditions forced the union to call a strike on August 25. About 3,000 men were now involved. On September 15 the union proposed joint control of the Shipping Office, but this was rejected. On September 30 the strike ended, the union being literally "starved into submission."

The Union in Defeat

The days following this disaster were hard ones for the sailors. Wages in some cases sank as low as $15. The Port Townsend Agency attempted to strike against the reduction, but San Francisco union headquarters refused to back the attempt. San Francisco was powerless to aid even had it wished. Discontent was rife within the ranks of its own membership, and finances were so precarious that it was even thought necessary to dispense with the telephone in the office. The membership in good standing fell off to about one-third, and many of the members had to go inland to secure work.

The years following the strike of 1886 were years of rebuilding the stricken union and laying the foundations for a greater effort to come. A year later the membership in good standing was only 1,436. The shortage of men on the coast, however, automatically forced wages to $40 in April, and in the following August wages rose to $45 to Humboldt Bay.

Union Ambitions

At this point in the union's history, the seamen discovered the policy which they have since pursued in realizing their ambitions. Founded amid the enthusiasm of socialist orators and vigorous young seamen, the union started out with high ideals and hopes of accomplishment, but with few ideas of means and methods beyond that of organization. Andrew Furuseth, who became secretary in 1887, set forth this situation in a letter to the members of his union written years afterwards.

DEAR COMRADES:

An organization of *men* lives on and by the ideal by which it is dominated. Ideals are to the individual and to the organization of men what salt is to fresh meat. Without it the meat is seized upon by maggots, is destroyed by them, and then the maggots die; with it the meat is preserved and remains useful. Our organization entered upon its life with some fairly well defined ideals as to what we wanted to do on this coast and elsewhere. We wanted to abolish the shipping master, the boarding master who mixed in the shipping of men, and the power of those forces in our lives. We wanted to reduce the power of the shipowner to legitimate proportions. We wanted to realize, not to destroy discipline. We wanted to learn to so conduct ourselves as to be able to reconquer our standing amongst our fellows as men and the standing of our calling. We did not know, or realize, what means we would have to employ. We had to make our own weapons as the fight progressed. . . . This organization, however, was never limited to the small number of seamen who find employment on this coast. Our aims had application to all the seamen of our race, and, therefore, we have steadily kept in mind that this coast was but a small part, and that, whatever success we might attain here, it would only be temporary, unless our ideals and our purposes could be extended to *all* seamen, not only in this country, but in Europe.

Legal Freedom and Economic Power

Early in 1887 the seamen began to be conscious of the social and economic significance of their status under the law. The law of 1874 had repealed all provisions of the law of 1872 in the coastwise and Lake trades, and in trade between the United States and British North American possessions. The unintended result was to give seamen in these trades (according to most courts) the power to desert without being arrested, detained, and surrendered back. (See Chapter VI for a more complete discussion of this matter.) This fact was ascertained in February, 1887, by Secretary Furuseth and reported to the membership. The union thereupon took advantage of the sailor's new legal position to conduct, not an open strike, but a sort of guerrilla warfare quite similar to what among shore workers would be called a "strike in detail." The men now fought the passport system by using it to get into the vessels, denying their union membership. Then, just as the vessel was ready to sail, they would come ashore causing the vessel delay while a new crew was secured. This was held lawful by most courts under the law of 1874, and ultimately resulted in the abolition of the grade book system. The men fought the boardinghouse combine by staying in the boardinghouses and running up bills.

Then, where they could, they refused to pay, although the boardinghouse keepers were at the pay table to get their money first. It was in this struggle that the seamen learned the meaning of legal freedom in terms of economic power.

By October, 1890, the membership in good standing had been built up to 3,159 and the funds in the treasury amounted to $36,000. Agencies were maintained at Eureka, San Pedro, San Diego, and Seattle. Business was rather dull, but the shipowners made no serious attempt to reduce wages below the standard union scale. The grade book system was abolished. But union and non-union men sailed together. Not until March 19, 1891, did the union feel strong enough to establish its own shipping office again.

Relations with Longshoremen and Steamship Sailors

In December, 1887, the coast seamen became involved in a strike in San Pedro when the Shipowners' Association discharged seamen working on wharves as longshoremen, in order to force them to sea where there was a scarcity of sailors. The rest of the seamen ashore struck with the 150 longshoremen, and about 60 sailors came off their vessels, forfeiting, as prescribed by law, some $3,000 in wages. The main object of the strike originally was to protect the men working longshore. But when the longshoremen after a couple of days voted to return to work, leaving the seamen out alone, it then became the seamen's object to force the discharge of the Shipowners' Association agent, and to conduct shipping through the union agent. In this they failed.

Trouble was continually experienced with both the longshoremen and the steamship sailors. The longshoremen tried to assume jurisdiction of the discharging of cargoes, which would of course confine the seamen to the work of navigation at sea. Clashes with the steamship-men arose over questions of manning and wages on steam schooners, and were not finally settled until the amalgamation of the two unions.

Federation of Seamen

The eyes of the seamen were turned toward the achievement of national and international federation of seafaring men, but this did not become an accomplished fact until 1892 when the National Seamen's Union was founded. However, Furuseth, Waterhouse, and Crangle were sent as delegates to the convention of the British Seamen's Union at Glasgow in 1890. They also visited and reported on the Lake, Atlantic, and Gulf Seamen's Unions.

Coast Seamen's Journal Founded

One of the most important single acts of the union was the foundation of the *Coast Seamen's Journal.* The union felt the need for publicity, both to plead its cause before the public and to keep its own membership together and informed, especially the latter. A committee of Hoff-meyer, Leder, Haist, Fuhrman, and Furuseth reported after careful investigation that they believed a weekly journal could be made a success, and the union overwhelmingly approved. The first issue was a four-page paper, appearing on November 2, 1887, with Xaver H. Leder as editor. Too much cannot be said of the importance of the work of the *Journal* on behalf of the union and the cause of seamen the world over. Today it ranks as one of the leading papers of organized labor.

Organization Among Steamshipmen

The wave of unionism which swept the San Francisco waterfront in the middle of the eighties did not subside with the organization of the Coast Seamen's Union in 1885. Two years earlier the firemen on the steamers that had begun to appear on the coast in competition with sailing vessels had organized. In September, 1884, the steamship cooks and waiters formed a union. Following a threatened reduction of wages by the Oregon Railway and Navigation Company (which never took place), one of their number, B. B. Carter, took it upon himself to call a meeting of steamship cooks and waiters in Humboldt Hall. The group was addressed by Haskell of the International Workmen's Association, J. McBride of the Iron Moulders' Union, J. B. Johnson of the Knights of Labor, and others. A membership roll was passed around and signed by 50. From this beginning grew the Steamshipmen's Protective Association, which by 1886 claimed nearly 500 members. Only the deck sailors on the steamers remained unorganized.

Now early in January, 1886, President Carter and Joseph Kelly, of the Steamshipmen's Protective Association, appeared before meetings of the coast seamen, that is, men in the coasting sailing ships, to urge the formation of a union of steamship sailors, "distinct of all the unions hitherto organized upon the waterfront." Nothing tangible came of this attempt, but in May an organization of steamship sailors did appear. Like the unions of coasting sailors and steamship cooks and waiters, it was spontaneous among the men themselves, although assisted and stimulated by labor leaders and enthusiasts ashore.

The Steamshipmen's Protective Union, as the new organization was called, grew out of a desire for better hours for the deck crews on the steamers. About 30 steamships, principally American, were engaged at that time in the coasting and offshore trade. All carried sail as well as steam, and were manned by white crews with the exception of two English and two American steamers crossing the Pacific to Australia, which carried sometimes white, sometimes Chinese, sometimes mixed crews, i.e., white sailors on deck and Chinese in the fire-room.

Hours and Conditions Aboard Steamers

At sea the larger passenger and cargo vessels carried quartermasters to steer, and sometimes lookouts, the men assigned to these duties working alternately, or "watch and watch," as it is called. Members of steamer crews not assigned to these duties came on deck at 5 A. M., generally to wash down and clean ship. They worked until 5 P.M., with an hour off for breakfast at 8, and another for dinner at 12. Occasionally, when due to make port during the night, which of course meant all hands on deck to make fast the vessel, some time off was given. When necessary to set or take in sail at night it was likewise all hands on deck, which meant broken sleep.

On sailing day the order was 5:30 A.M., wash down and clean ship; breakfast, 6:30; back to work at 7; on the way to sea secure all cargo gear and deck cargo, mooring lines, closing hatches, etc., set sail, if necessary; then go below until the next day, or until nearing the next port, as the case might be. On other days in port, hours were 7 to 12 and 1 to 6, except the day before sailing, which often meant working as late as 9 P.M. loading cargo. Hours on Sundays and holidays in port were at the discretion of the first officer. Some officers were very considerate, others kept their men working until 10, 11, 12, and even 2 o'clock. It was in a spirit of protest against these hours and conditions, which had prevailed roughly between 1883 and 1886, that the steamship sailors now came together. It was natural and easy that they should unite to voice their common demand. The spirit of unionism was in the air in those days. All those about them were organized or organizing. The firemen and cooks and waiters had organized. Only the year before the coasting sailors, to the surprise of the owners, the public, the shore workers, and even the seamen themselves, had founded a union that was waging an apparently successful fight for existence. The International Workmen's Association (the Red), founded by Karl Marx, was represented in San Francisco by a group of enthusiasts whose ambition was to organize as many trades as possible. Perhaps chief among these was Burnette G. Haskell, a young lawyer of magnetic personality and a persuasive speaker. Not a laboring man by birth or training, he had nevertheless become an ardent worker for the betterment of the working classes. It was he, who with a few other organizers from the International, had played such a prominent part in aiding and stimulating the organization of the Coast Seamen's Union and had fired the zeal of the cooks and waiters with his oratory. So when in May the steamshipmen gathered in little groups along the wharves to discuss the demand for better hours, and an organization to enforce it, Haskell again appeared on the waterfront to fire the enthusiasm of the sailors to organize for their own protection and uplift. An informal meeting was held on the Broadway dock, and it was decided to form a union. Among those present there were many who already belonged to the Coast Seamen's Union, others who had been to sea but were now working ashore, but all united in the new Steamship Sailors' Protective Union of the Pacific Coast. The owners sent representatives to the union to inform the men that they were entirely willing to listen to the requests of the men, and granted not only the original demand for no work after 6 P.M., but voluntarily agreed to limit the hours of work in port to between 7 and 5 to conform to the hours worked in the engine and steward's departments.

Jurisdictional Disputes

The new union joined the Federated Trades and Labor Organizations of the Pacific Coast and sent delegates to the Council in San Francisco. They remained but for a short time. Although the two seamen's unions were friendly at the outset, they soon came to disagreement. There was continual wrangling over which should supply the crew for the steam schooners that carried both steam and sail. With two unions in a single field, such struggles for jurisdiction were bound to arise and they continued incessantly until the unions were finally amalgamated. On October 14, 1887, the Steamshipmen's Union was expelled from the Federated Trades. It was charged that under the leadership of Dave McDonald, secretary, the steamshipmen had endeavored to extend their jurisdiction at the expense of the sailors, refusing all offers of co-operation and amalgamation, and that steamshipmen had underbid and taken the places of coast seamen.

In 1889 an incipient strike of the steamshipmen took place over hours and conditions. The steamship companies had begun the habit of giving the men tickets good for 37 cents a day at certain restaurants instead of feeding the men aboard ship when the vessels were in port. Both the amount allowed and the particular restaurants were obnoxious to the men. The union protested and compelled the companies to give an allowance of 20 cents a meal, and to leave the men free to eat where they chose. Before the organization of the union the men, with a few exceptions, had worked late Sunday forenoon and occasionally into the afternoon when the vessel was in port, scraping and painting and cleaning. The union cut this down to two hours—7 to 9—for washing the decks. In addition, it maintained wages of steamshipmen $5 a month above those paid to sailors on sailing vessels. The early steamshipmen, unlike the men in sailing vessels, did not have to fight the crimps, for the masters of steamers customarily shipped crews either directly or through the union office. Neither were they obliged to resist the introduction of Orientals, for the coasting steamers never tried to carry Chinese crews, as did some of the sailers. In these respects, as well as in matters of hours and wages, the steamshipmen were in a more advantageous position than their fellows who manned the windjammers.

In February, 1890, the steamshipmen walked out on account of trouble in the boats running to Portland, Oregon. The strike lasted but one day, ending in submission to the company's demands.

The union maintained, besides the office in San Francisco, a branch in Seattle. In 1889 they organized the steamboatmen on Puget Sound to the number of about three or four hundred. These branches became part of the Sailors' Union of the Pacific when the amalgamation took place, but soon after disintegrated during the panic of 1893.

On December 13, 1889, the Steamship Sailors' Union was readmitted to the Federated Trades. But trouble again caused a breach between the steamshipmen and the Coast Seamen's Union. The Coast Seamen's Union demanded that exchange books should be issued between the two unions, allowing members of each union employment on either steam or sailing vessels. The steamshipmen refused on the ground that they were free to ship on steamers through their own union office or direct with the masters; but if they tried to ship on sailing vessels under the proposed exchange system, they would have to put themselves in the power of the crimping boarding masters who still controlled shipping on sailing vessels. The Federated Trades, however, upheld the Coast Seamen, and on April 4, 1890, the Steamshipmen's Union withdrew from the Federated Trades. Shortly afterwards the steamshipmen, feeling the need of outside affiliation, took the lead in organizing the City Front Labor Council.

Amalgamation

Ernest Lea, L. Lazaravich, an Australian of Slavic descent; Daniel Dunn, a native of Ireland, and John Coleman, later a mate on the coast, successively followed Dave McDonald as secretary of the steamshipmen's union. In 1890 and 1891 sentiment favoring amalgamation with the Coast Seamen's Union grew stronger as the futility of fighting each other became more apparent and the hold of the crimps on the sailors grew weaker. The steamshipmen proposed amalgamation on equal terms under a new name and constitution, and on February 2, 1891, the coast seamen agreed. A series of joint meetings was held debating the proposition and the means of accomplishing it. The difficulties in the way were many, one of which was that the steamshipmen were incorporated. Not until July 29, 1891, were the two unions finally amalgamated under the name of the Sailors' Union of the Pacific. It was under the leadership of Nicholas Jortall, then secretary, that the steamshipmen were finally persuaded to vote for union. The steamshipmen brought to the new union a membership of about 1,000 and a treasury of $13,000. This gave the Sailors' Union of the Pacific a membership of between 3,500 and 4,000 in good standing and a treasury of over $50,000, making it probably the strongest labor union local in the country at that time. The losses of the strike of 1886 had been more than made up, and the union now began final preparations for a great effort by which they hoped to wrest the control of shipping from the Shipowners' and Coasting Boarding Masters' Associations, and to abolish finally the abuses which had pursued the sailor wherever he went.

Knights of Labor

Another attempted organization of seamen seems worthy of mention in passing. The Knights of Labor, through the efforts of Von Hoffmeyer of the Musicians' Union, tried to organize a Neptune Assembly about 1888. The membership was only about 150 and the Assembly soon died a natural death in a field already more than occupied by the Steamshipmen's Union and the Coast Seamen's Union.

CHAPTER V

SAILORS VS. SHIPOWNERS: THE INDUSTRIAL FIELD[1]

The Sailors' Union in 1891

The reorganized union started out with good prospects. The membership was strong, the treasury filled, and working conditions satisfactory for that time. Sailors in coasting steamers were working a 54-hour week for a monthly wage of $40, with work on Sundays and holidays paid for at the rate of 40 cents an hour. The system of grade books, or passports, instituted by the Shipowners' Association in 1886, had been abolished and the union had established a shipping office to further break the power of the boarding masters. Some informal agreements were maintained with a few shipowners, regulating wages, hours, and conditions, and providing for preference in employment to union sailors. Correspondence was being exchanged with the Eastern, Lake, and Gulf unions with a view to the formation of a National Union of Seamen. In February, 1891, a federation of waterfront unions called the City Front Labor Council, had been formed at the instigation of the steamshipmen, and

---

[1] Sources for the information in this chapter are:
Files of San Francisco newspapers (see page 16).
Reports of Commissioner of Navigation (see page 3).
Sailors' Union of the Pacific.
  Constitution and By-Laws. San Francisco, 1919.
  Minutes, including record of meetings, reports of officers and committees, and various letters to the union, or written by officers of the union on official business, 1891——. (Not open to public inspection. Access to records 1891–1919 granted to writer during preparation of this work.)
  Wages and Working Rules. San Francisco, 1922.
Eaves, Lucile. A history of California Labor Legislation, with an introductory sketch of the San Francisco labor movement. Berkeley, 1910.

the Sailors' Union had united with the other unions in
this movement. Besides the headquarters in San Francisco, branches of the Sailors' Union were maintained in
Seattle, Port Townsend, Portland, Eureka, San Pedro,
and San Diego, where union meetings were regularly held
and union agents stationed to keep ships supplied with
union crews, and to look out for union interests generally.

Sailors and Longshoremen

But the prosperity was only temporary. Trouble soon
broke out among the unions themselves. In August, the
longshoremen of Port Pirie, Australia, requested the
sailors not to sign to discharge cargo—a request impossible of fulfilment since the form of articles is prescribed
by law—and the San Francisco longshoremen requested
the sailors not to work overtime on the wharves. Here
was the old conflict of jurisdiction which has existed on
the coast since the founding of sailors' and longshoremen's unions. The sailors felt that the longshoremen
were trying to deprive them of work which rightfully
belonged to them.

In December, 1891, longshoremen refused to take lumber from the union crew of the "Annie Larson," claimed
the work for themselves, and compelled the captain to
discharge the crew. The breach widened, and when the
longshoremen struck the following March, the seamen
refused their request not to discharge cargo except to
union longshoremen. To accede might cost the sailors
their own wages as forfeit, and involve their union in a
strike upon which they had taken no vote. So they
asserted that they would discharge cargo to anyone regardless of union affiliation. It was not long before the
City Front Labor Council, composed of such discordant

elements, succumbed to the jealousies and rivalries of its members.

Business Depression

Nor were serious difficulties with the shipowners slow to arise. It was in the days preceding the panic of 1893. Business was slackening, freights were falling, and the owners were desirous of reducing wages. In November, 1891, the shipowners demanded a 25 per cent reduction in wages. For some months the union resisted successfully in spite of the fact that there were estimated to be 1,800 non-union seamen in San Francisco, including deepwater men and whalers, and that during the winter of 1891–1892 there were 600 to 700 union men ashore. But serious trouble lay ahead, and the union knew that the struggle over wages involved the more vital question of the control over shipping seamen. Throughout the spring and early summer of 1892 "scabbing" became increasingly prevalent, and increasingly a menace to the union. In the Honolulu trade shipment of non-union men was almost general. In addition to the excess of seamen already on shore the crimps brought in deep-water sailors to take the places of the union men in coasting vessels.

Sailors vs. Shipowners

By June, 1892, the fight was on in earnest. One of the owners proposed a reduction of wages. The union refused to accept, and appropriated $3,000 to "stop scabbing." The efforts of the owners to man their ships with non-union crews kept the waterfront in turmoil for months following. In order to get such crews safely aboard, the aid of the police was regularly invoked. Many of the non-union crews were furnished from the Sailors' Home operated by the Ladies' Seamen's Friend

Society, whose relations with organized seamen have been discussed in earlier chapters.

In August the union authorized its executive committee to call union men out of all vessels of owners who carried non-union crews on any of their ships going to the Hawaiian Islands. For a time union men underbid "scabs" so as to keep the latter out of jobs, the union paying the difference in wages in a vain endeavor to check the undermining of union control. In order to maintain the coast rates, men were encouraged to ship on deep-water vessels, in an effort on the part of the union to counteract the activities of the boarding masters who were trying to ship deep-water men at reduced rates on the coast. The coasting trade was the battle-ground for contending parties. Attempt was also made to enforce the laws against advance wages and against crimping, which the union alleged were being violated in the struggle to supply "scabs."

Violence on the Waterfront

The struggle dragged on through the remainder of 1892, and was marked by considerable violence to person and property. Some owners still shipped union crews. But when the Shipowners' Association shipped non-union men, as it regularly did, there was usually a disturbance on the waterfront. In one of the fights Otto Anderson, a union sailor, was stabbed to death by a non-unionist. Frequently the owners complained of such depredations as the cutting of ropes and hawsers, setting vessels adrift, and even the sawing of anchor chains. By the first of the year the Shipowners' Association, tiring of the fight, was about ready to give up. But the Manufacturers' and Employers' Association of California, which was active in breaking up unions, took hold of the shipowners' struggle, and detailed G. C. Williams to renew the fight. Williams was made secretary of the Shipowners' Association, and in January, 1893, he assumed charge of operations against the union.

Shipowners Renew Activities

The law of August 19, 1890, passed at the instance of the shipowners, had applied the penal clauses of the Shipping Commissioners' Act to seamen in the coasting trade shipped before a United States Shipping Commissioner without granting them the protection and privileges of that act. Previous to this time no actual injustice had been worked, because the sailors had refused to ship before a Commissioner. But now under Williams' leadership, the owners took advantage of the situation to compel men to ship before a Commissioner. Thus they were brought under the penal clauses of the law of 1890, which included, among other things, arrest for desertion. A shipping office was opened, and a Deputy United States Shipping Commissioner was secured to be in constant attendance at the owners' shipping office. The deputy was probably little more than an agent for the shipowners, since he received only 25 cents a day from the government, although nearly all shipments in San Francisco were made before the deputy in the shipowners' office.

Under this stimulus, the number of crews shipped before the Commissioner in the coastwise and adjacent trade rose from 193 men, furnished to 18 vessels, for the first half of 1892 (before the strike) to 1,486 men furnished to 265 vessels in the first half of 1893. With very few exceptions these men were shipped before the deputy at the association office, which is clear proof of the shipowners' success and their reliance on the penal clauses of the law of 1890. To quote the United States Shipping Commissioner at San Francisco:

This large volume of business compared with that of former years in this class of vessels is most encouraging, and indicates a growing favorable opinion among the owners of coastwise vessels that they can best subserve their interests, protect their property, and discipline and control their crews by taking advantage of the law of August 19, 1890, and sign their crews before this office.

That the penalty of imprisonment for desertion as reintroduced in the coastwise trade under the law of 1890 was no mere dead letter but was intended for use and proved effective in time of strike is further indicated by the following news item appearing in the San Francisco *Examiner* of February 21, 1893:

Desertions are quite common at present, and the boarding-house men and captains are prosecuting such of the runaways as they can get their hands on. Several United States officers made a roundup on the waterfront this morning and caught three of half a dozen recalcitrant men they had warrants for.

The struggle took on the character of an effort to wear out the other side financially. Williams endeavored to ship crews as cheaply as possible. Japanese, farmers, and cowboys, as well as sailors, were used to man the ships. An alliance was entered into with the boarding masters, whereby the Shipowners' Association paid advance wages on sailors' board bills, and in return the boarding masters furnished non-union men to the shipping office without demanding blood money. The men endeavored to make the shipment of non-union crews as expensive as possible as well as to prevent them from being taken aboard. Union men shipped as ostensibly non-union men, and then left the vessel at the moment of departure, in order to cause costly delay in demurrage and the securing of a new crew; and efforts were made to prevent the securing and placing aboard of non-union

crews. The owners countered by invoking the law of
1890 to return deserters to their ships.

In a letter of instructions to his Seattle agent, later
printed in the San Francisco *Examiner,* Williams outlined the policy to be followed in conducting the campaign for the shipowners:

> The main object in the administration of affairs is to save
> expense to the shipowner. . . . The line of tactics adopted by
> the union is to make the cost to the shipowner as much as pos-
> sible. Their hope is to wear the shipowner out through the
> pocket. The problem of the association is to prevent the fight
> from costing the shipowner too much.
>
> The real problem in this fight is a financial one. If the asso-
> ciation can be run at a small expense to the shipowner, every
> vessel will soon be placed upon its register and there will be no
> union because there will be no vessels for the union sailors to
> man. . . .
>
> Never have a union agent arrested, except for some offense
> that the State is bound to prosecute, and which does not require
> the employment of a special attorney to represent the associa-
> tion. . . .
>
> A man might be justified in shooting any number of men who
> board a vessel with felonious intent, while the same man would
> not be justified at all in indulging in a wordy quarrel on the
> street. A dose of cold lead has a wonderful effect in quieting
> disorders if it is only given in the right time and in the right
> place, whereas a dose of cold lead at the wrong time and in the
> wrong place would merely create a riot.
>
> By your entire conduct create the impression upon both the
> union men and the community in general that your greatest
> desire is to preserve peace; that you will do anything to avoid
> a conflict, that you will submit to any indignity without retaliat-
> ing; but that when it becomes necessary to guard the property
> of the association you will not hesitate to kill. Once you obtain
> that reputation you will discover that you have far less trouble
> and the work of your agency will run along smoothly.

The union resisted the owners to the limit of its ability. By the end of March only about 300 union men
were ashore, the rest having gone into fishing vessels or
inland in search of employment. The board of members
and sometimes of non-union sailors out of employment
was paid by the union to keep them from the necessity of
"scabbing," this item of expense amounting to as high

as $1,000 a week. Salaries of officers were cut one-half, and the waterfront was patrolled. The wage scale in vessels whose owners had kept agreements with the union throughout the strike was reduced $5 a month, with the consent of the union. The situation was bad for the union, with no relief in sight so long as business remained stagnant and unemployment so general.

Union Defeat

During the latter part of August, 1893, the union had so far lost the fight that the association, now comprised of about 45 owners, reinstituted the old grade book system of 1886–1887 to clinch their hold on the shipment of sailors. All men shipping on association vessels were now required to carry the association grade book which bore a description of the man, and upon which each master recorded the seaman's qualifications. Already the men were defeated, in spite of the fact that they refused to acknowledge it. Against the continued depression they were powerless to resist the owners.

On the 25th of September came the final blow. An explosion of a valise containing dynamite in front of Curtin's non-union sailor boardinghouse, which caused considerable damage to both life and property, was laid at the door of the union. Public feeling ran high against the sailors as the newspapers and the Shipowners' Association played up the affair to the detriment of the union. Williams recited in the newspapers the acts of violence to persons and property which had occurred on the waterfront, charging the union with at least incitement to the violence committed by members or sympathizers in its behalf, and ended by denouncing the Sailors' Union as an "anarchistic society." The sentiment of the Shipowners' Association was reported in the papers to be

for crushing the union out of existence. In a circular
the Manufacturers' and Employers' Association made the
following pronouncement:

The Manufacturers' and Employers' Association can look with
complacency upon its work during the last two years. One
after another the unions have been taught a salutary lesson until
out of the horde of unions only one or two are left of any
strength. This association has taken hold of the shipowners
struggle and it is only a question of time when the Sailors'
Union will have gone the way of the rest. It is of most vital
importance that this good work should go on. Trade unionism
among workmen is like tares in the field of wheat. The word and
the act should be placed among the things prohibited by law.

In its editorial columns the *Examiner* demanded, "Let
the Coast Seamen's Union hunt down the murderers, not
for the Governor's reward, but for its own vindication."
Goodall and Perkins, who had been carrying union crews,
took the occasion to terminate their agreement with the
union. Still more vessels were being laid up on account
of the business situation. Further resistance was useless, so on October 16, 1893, the seamen capitulated,
voting the resolution usual in such cases, that union members shall sail "for what can be obtained."

The perpetrator of the Curtin dynamite outrage has
never been found. The union has always maintained its
innocence, and as soon as the explosion happened offered
a reward of $1,000 for the conviction of the guilty party.
Several union men were arrested; one of them, John
Tyrrel, was tried, but not convicted. Union members of
that time maintain the belief that the dynamite was
"planted" as part of a plan to discredit the union. John
Curtin, Jr., who was injured by the blast, stated that he
had warned the sailor who picked up the valise, just before the explosion, "It may be full of dynamite!" and
had started to run. This lends color to the latter theory,

but the truth of the matter has never been authoritatively determined.

Union Surrender

The defeat of the union was complete and well-nigh crushing. The membership was cut to 1,650, one-half of the strength with which the union had started, and it rapidly fell off in the hard times that followed to about one-quarter of the original strength. The funds in the treasury were likewise diminished by one-half, and in the months following fell almost to nothing. Wages were down to $20, half of what they were in 1891; they were set by the owners without even a semblance of union control for a long time to come. Severe as was their defeat, the sailors accepted it, but took as their watchword the motto: "Tomorrow is also a day."

For a year following their surrender, the seamen made no move to raise wages; it would have been useless had they tried. Their membership steadily fell off, and likewise the funds in their treasury. In July, 1894, the membership in good standing was 908, and some $14,000 was the extent of the funds remaining. But in October, 1894, emboldened by an increase of about 300 in the membership, the sailors felt that conditions warranted them in demanding an increase in wages to $30 to inside ports. A long-drawn-out struggle ensued, lasting through the winter of 1894 and the first half of 1895. But there were too many non-union men on the coast, shipping was too dull, and the treasury, now dwindled to $4,000, was too depleted to withstand the steady drain upon it. The fight to maintain wages at the union level was unsuccessful and had to be abandoned. During the strike an attempt was made to abolish the *Coast Seamen's Journal* because it was requiring some financial aid from the union at a time when it could least afford to give it. Fortunately, however, the majority was made to realize that at just such a time the *Journal* was needed most of all, and the paper was continued.

The history of the next three or four years of union effort on the industrial field is a story of almost continual struggle to keep up the membership of the union, to keep "scabbing" down to a minimum, and to hold wages up as well as possible. Slowly improving business conditions were on the side of the men, but the Shipowners' Association and the plentiful number of non-union sailors available limited the union efforts to the most indifferent success.

CHAPTER VI

SAILORS VS. SHIPOWNERS: THE POLITICAL FIELD[1]

The Question of Navigation Laws

The years 1891–1898 were years of complete failure for the Sailors' Union in the industrial field. The economic power of the organization had been wholly shattered, and the membership and treasury were but a fraction of what they had been in 1891. Nevertheless these were years of achievement in another direction which overbalanced the losses sustained in the industrial field.

Attention has already been drawn to the special significance of the peculiar and unfree legal status of the sailor. For the removal of this barrier to social and economic progress, for the abolition of the crimping system by law, the seamen's leaders now turned their attention to legislation. In order to understand these efforts, it is necessary to review briefly the laws relating to seamen.

The body of our navigation laws which has given statutory effect to or modified the old maritime law really dates from 1872. The act of July 20, 1790, provided for the apprehension of deserters on justices' warrants, and contained a fugitive seaman's clause with penalties for

---

[1] Sources for this chapter are: Records of congressional hearings, Reports of Commissioner of Navigation, United States Statutes (Boston and Washington, 1850———). Also:
  Macarthur, Walter, comp. The Seaman's Contract, 1790-1918; a complete reprint of the laws relating to American seamen, enacted, amended, and repealed . . . . as originally published in the Statutes at Large. Compiled and arranged for purposes of comparison. San Francisco, 1919.

harboring deserters.   But aside from that law, and the
laws of 1835 and 1850 dealing with corporal punishment
and flogging, no laws had been enacted which vitally affected the status of the seaman.

In 1872 what is known as the Shipping Commissioner's Act became law, establishing the office of Shipping Commissioner to superintend all shipping agreements, and defining in great detail the signing on and
discharge of seamen, and their relation to the ship, the
owner, and the officers, with penalties for desertion, and
many other provisions relating to their legal rights and
duties.   How this law failed to curb shanghaiing because
evaded by the crimps has already been told in Chapter II.

Act of 1874

At first the act applied to seamen in all trades.   But
two years later, by the amendment of June 9, 1874, it was
decreed that none of the provisions of the Shipping Commissioner's Act should apply to the coastwise and lake-
going trade.   Since the Shipping Commissioner's Act was
practically a codification of pre-existing law and governed
the seaman in nearly all of his personal relations with his
employers, the question arose, if this act did not apply to
coastwise trade, what law did?   Some courts held that
since the law of 1872 was chiefly a re-enactment of previously existing law, the amendment of 1874 was practically without effect, except as to features enacted for the
first time in the law of 1872.   Most courts, however, construed the amendment literally, and if the particular case
was found to be covered by a clause in the Shipping Commissioner's Act, it was held for that reason not to apply
to the coastwise trade.   This difficulty has been partly
remedied, but for some time there was confusion over the

interpretation, and as to whether the amendment of 1874 applied to later amendments of the act of 1872.

Unintended Effect of Act of 1874

The significance to sailors of the act of 1874 was this. According to the view of the majority of courts, every provision of the act of 1872 relating to coastwise vessels, including the sections concerning crimes and offenses, was stricken out. The effect was to abolish the penalty for desertion in the coastwise trade—an effect not in the minds of the congressmen when the act was passed. There was practically nothing said about the bill in House or Senate except that it was intended to relieve the owners of vessels in short coastwise runs between ports in two adjoining states or between Maine and New Brunswick who had been subjected to the inconvenient necessity of signing the crew on under shipping articles and paying them off for each short run, even though it might be for only 10 miles. That the abolition of the penalty for desertion was the practical effect of the law was first ascertained by Secretary Furuseth in 1887. It meant, according to most courts, that coasting seamen were free men. In Chapter IV we saw how this freedom enabled the seamen to resist the shipowners. The tactics of delaying the vessel by suddenly going ashore at the moment of intended departure finally brought about the abolition of the owners' shipping office, and broke their control over the employment of sailors. The shipowners were for the time being without their customary legal protection against a sudden strike, protection which had long since been denied to the factory and mill owners ashore as a violation of the workers' rights as free men. This is the practical significance to the seaman of his struggle for freedom.

Protests Against Sailors

This period of freedom, however, was soon ended. The protests which arose over the seamen's use of their liberty caught the ear of the Commissioner of Navigation and were echoed approvingly by him. He recited cases of desertion and refusal to serve after signing articles which the courts, under the law of 1874, were refusing to punish. Even in the case of a seaman convicted of a brutal and atrocious assault upon a master, the court had held that judgment must be arrested because of the law of 1874. This latter instance was obviously a miscarriage of justice, and lent added strength to the cries of protest. In the Commissioner's report for 1889, the Oregon state law against desertion was printed by way of suggestion and as a "matter of interest" to shipowners. And under the caption "Seamen Shirking Duty" a decision in the case of two union seamen was reprinted as a further argument for re-enacting punishments for seamen in the coastwise trade to aid discipline and compel the specific performance of seamen's contracts. It was also in substantiation of a charge that: "In many cases the supply and the quality of the seamen are affected by the operations of the sailors' unions, especially on the Pacific coast." It appeared from the decision that a letter to one of the seamen, which the court accepted as genuine, had been written by "the secretary or agent of the 'Coast Seamen's union,' H. Furwell [A. Furuseth?]." The letter informed the men:

You have your medicen, though, first in the coals and then at anything which comes along. You know as long as you make an effort, no matter how small, he can do nothing. If only 25 tons of coal get out per day you are doing as much as you can, you know; and that settles it.

In taking in sails you may be an hour to do what could be done in five minutes. You may be four hours hoisting a top-sail, and he can do nothing; if his sails blow away you can not help it, and so forth. You know pretty well how to do that anyhow.

The court, in commenting on this policy, stated:

I am strongly impressed with the idea that the whole trouble grows out of the methods and purposes of the Seamen's Union of San Francisco. It appears to be organized for the purpose of controlling the conduct and employment of seamen on this coast, to the end that ships shall be navigated in the interest and at the pleasure of the forecastle, without any reference to the rights or interests of owners.

Acting on this anarchical idea, these libelants undertook to administer to the master the prescribed "medicine" for his refusal to submit to their dictation, by loitering and trifling over their work in discharging cargo at the expense of the ship.

Act of 1890

In response to this situation depicted by the Commissioner of Navigation, which combined protests against desertion, crime, "soldiering," and the alleged baneful influence of the union, Congress passed the act of August 19, 1890. By the act of 1872 the rights and duties of seamen had been carefully laid down to apply to all seamen. In 1874 seamen in the coastwise trade were exempted. Now came the provision that if a seaman in the coastwise trade shipped in the presence of a shipping commissioner, he was subject to the punitive clauses of the act of 1872 and yet was denied the privileges and advantages secured to him under that same act. Such was the effect of the act of 1890, which, with the exception of two or three clauses prescribing the manner and form of making contracts, applied penalties only, such as one day's pay for each hour of tardiness in reporting for duty, arrest by the master without warrant, imprisonment for desertion, and $10 a day fine for harboring a deserter.

Of course, legally the sailors were not obliged to ship under this severe law. But in 1893 the Shipowners' Association determined to make the provisions of the act effective. Against the resistance of the Sailors' Union in a prolonged strike, it compelled the seamen on the Pacific coast to ship through its office before a deputy shipping commissioner in order to invoke the penalties of the act of 1890, including imprisonment for desertion. Thus the seamen lost the freedom which they had temporarily enjoyed.

Seamen Aware of Importance of Law

In the meantime, however, the seamen's leaders had become fully conscious of the importance of laws relating to sailors, and were preparing to work for the repeal of the act of 1890 even before it was actually invoked against them. They also knew, as did nearly everyone else, that it was the payment of advance wages and allotments that made crimping profitable. When these payments had been curtailed by the law of 1884, the crimps had held up the vessels until the owners or masters paid them in spite of the law, and two years later, in recognition of the power of the crimps, the law was repealed. The union leaders now determined to re-enact the prohibition against advance and allotment, and to rely upon the vigilance of the union to secure the enforcement of the prohibition.

Committee on Maritime Law

In January, 1892, a committee on maritime law was elected to prepare a legislative program for the union. The active members of this committee, Frank Waterhouse, Ed Crangle, George Bolton, George M. Lynch, and Nicholas Jortall, studied the laws of several other nations, making their own translations. They then drew up bills modeled after these patterns and forwarded them to United States Senator Frye, of the Committee on Commerce, and to the Commissioner of Navigation as an "Appeal to Congress."

The same year it became known that Judge James G. Maguire had aspirations to go to Congress from the Fourth Congressional District, comprising the waterfront of San Francisco. The Sailors' Union hearing of his aspirations, and having confidence in him because of his record on the bench, sent a committee to ask his stand on the bill they had drawn up. Judge Maguire, after considering the bill, sent word that he endorsed it, and if elected would work for its adoption. The union thereupon endorsed Maguire's candidacy, regarding its endorsement not as an entry of the union into politics, but as a step toward the improvement of the status of seamen. The sailors canvassed every house in the district with the result that in November Maguire was elected to Congress.

In the meantime nothing had come of the seamen's bills. And nothing did come of their "Appeal to Congress" until January, 1894, when it was introduced in the House by Judge Maguire in a series of bills which henceforth were known as the Maguire bills. On March 6, 1894, Andrew Furuseth, secretary of the Sailors' Union, was sent to Washington to work for the bills. In his report to the National Seamen's Union of America, Furuseth said:

We found the predominant feeling among the members of the Committee, and indeed among those of the general membership of Congress to whom we spoke on the subject, to be that American seamen were better treated on the whole than seamen of any other nation. But with the material proofs at our command we were able to make a very decided alteration in that traditional sentiment. . . .

As a general rule I found the Democrats and Populist members of both houses in favor of our bills and the Republicans opposed. General Bingham, whom we must regard as the chief opponent of the bills, is a republican and is avowedly working in the interest of the Cramps [shipbuilding firm] of Philadelphia.

Maguire Act

The bills went to the House Committee on Merchant Marine and Fisheries, and Bill 5603 was reported out favorably, the other bills having been held up in the subcommittee. The report cited the effects of the act of 1890 in applying only punitive sections of the act of 1872 to coastwise seamen, made compulsory upon Pacific coast seamen by exercise of the power of the Shipowners' Association of that coast. When the bill was reported on the floor of the House, General Bingham by filibustering tactics consumed the committee's hour and forced postponement of the bill's consideration. But its friends were later able to muster enough votes to bring it up and secure its passage. On February 18, 1895, the Maguire Act became law. By excluding certain sections of the Revised Statutes it in effect repealed the act of 1890, abolished imprisonment for desertion in the coastwise trade, abolished allotment either to relatives (used as a subterfuge by the crimps) or to an "original creditor" (crimp) in the coastwise trade, extended certain protective provisions of the Shipping Commissioner's Act to seamen in the coastwise trade shipped before commissioners, and by the proviso added on the floor by Dingley of Maine, to the seamen's own bill, exempted seamen's clothing from attachment under penalty of fine. This proviso came as a result of conference between Frye and Dingley, both of Maine, and Andrew Furuseth, held in the Hamilton Hotel while the bill was being considered in the House. To make this last proviso even more effective against the crimps, in 1904 holding of seamen's clothing was declared to be a misdemeanor.

The Maguire Act was hailed as a great victory by the seamen, for it broke the power of the crimps in the coastwise trade and was the first great step toward their goal

of a freeman's status. But they were not content to rest
on their oars. With the opening of the 54th session of
Congress the International Seamen's Union was back with
the Maguire bills that had failed of passage the previous
session. Furuseth was again sent to Washington. This
time he was aided by Adolf Strasser of the American
Federation of Labor and the Atlantic and Great Lakes
Unions. Although no very important legislation for
sailors was passed by this Congress, the hearings on the
bills brought out some illuminating facts concerning the
issues and alignments in the contest.

The seamen's bills in the House were referred to the
Committee on Merchant Marine and Fisheries before
whom those interested pro and con appeared to testify in
January and February, 1896. The religious welfare organizations, the owners, the crimps (who appeared under
the more dignified name of shipping masters), and the
seamen were all represented before the committee. The
seamen were asking for the total abolition of advance and
allotment; for the abolition of imprisonment for desertion
in all trades, not merely the coastwise as provided by the
Maguire Act, contending that forfeiture of wages and
personal effects was sufficient penalty for the breach of a
civil contract; for measures making the vessel itself liable
in damages for brutalities inflicted by officers; and for
improved food scales and forecastle spaces.

Opposition to Seamen's Bills

A few quotations from the hearings are the very best
evidence of the source, nature, and extent of the opposition encountered by the seamen. The Rev. George W.
M'Laughlin of Philadelphia, secretary of the Seamen's
Society, which for half a century had proclaimed as its

purpose the progress and uplift of the sailor, testified as
follows:

Having somewhat of a humanitarian side to my nature, and
knowing the purposes and objects of those organizations, I ought
to comprehend the bearings of this proposed law. Years ago I
was in very close sympathy with no advance, but I have been
forced from circumstances and nothing else, to change my mind.
If sailors were like any other class of men it would not be so
difficult to handle them . . . the facts of their lives prove that
without any further statement, they being cut off from all social
relations with their fellowmen two-thirds of their lives, and hence
in legislation for them you are compelled to abide their necessities,
therefore a law should exist and aid that class of men. . . .
My business has been to study the character of the sailor, and I
can say that he has lost his self-respect to an extent that is
wonderful. He has become a mendicant. . . . He has sim-
plicity of character when on shore; but he is disposed to be
improvident. . . . If there is no advance, tell me how will that
man go to sea without credit? How is it possible to reinstate him
in his calling?

Apparently the seamen's friends did not sense the
fact, which almost everyone else knew, that the crimps
fed upon the sailor's advance, and that it was they who
were largely responsible for his destitution. Only the
year before the Commissioner of Navigation had stated
in his annual report that for the year, as against 732 allotments to relatives, there were 15,503 to "original creditors," and added, "The allotments are almost invariably
made out in favor of boardinghouse keepers." One is
forced to the conclusion that the seaman knew his own
plight and the remedy therefor better than anyone else.
Yet when he sought to lift himself out of it, he found
himself alone, with his professed friends in strange alliance against him.

Views of Opponents of Bills

The testimony of R. R. Freeman, secretary of the
Vessel Owners' Association, Mr. Sharwood, secretary of
the Philadelphia Maritime Exchange, and Vernon C.

Brown, president of the Maritime Exchange of New York, representing owners, and Mr. James A. O'Brien, a shipping master (or, according to the Seamen's Union, a crimp) of Philadelphia, throws much light on the character and reasons for opposition to abolition of advance and allotment.

MR. FURUSETH: Is it the position the owners take at the present time that advance or allotment is a necessity for the owners?

MR. FREEMAN: The position that owners take is that they cannot get a crew unless allotment is paid in certain portions of the country. The system of refusing allotments has been tried once and would not work. . . .

MR. FURUSETH: Then the allotment system is a benefit to the owner?

MR. FREEMAN: He gets a crew when he wants it.

And similarly:

MR. FURUSETH: Does the Philadelphia Maritime Association claim that an allotment is necessary in order to obtain men?

MR. SHARWOOD: Yes, the Philadelphia Maritime Exchange are of the opinion that an allotment to seamen is necessary.

MR. FURUSETH: In order to obtain seamen?

MR. SHARWOOD: In order to obtain seamen.

And then on the side of the crimps:

MR. FURUSETH: What do you refer to as doing what others do, you mean under ordinary conditions you have got to return to the vessel or to the owner or to the captain, as the case may be, on your allotment note, a certain amount of that allotment note?

MR. O'BRIEN: That is it. . . .

MR. FURUSETH: And as a general proposition you pay over something from that allotment as a margin to the master of the vessel?

MR. O'BRIEN: I could hardly say generally, because I do not think I would call it general; but very often.

And Mr. O'Brien agreed that the law of 1884 abolishing advance and allotment for two years was a "miserable failure." Of course it was, for the crimps tied up all the vessels and forced the owners to evade the law. It is all very clear—the crimps refused to supply or allow crews to go aboard unless they could mortgage the sailors' wages; the owners wanted crews and preferred to pay advance rather than risk another encounter with the crimps; and besides this, the captains often shared the allotment with the crimp.

Shipowners on Imprisonment for Desertion

The testimony of Vernon C. Brown is interesting on the attitude of his association of owners toward seamen. In protesting against a provision of one of the Maguire bills that 24 hours' notice of a seaman's refusal to serve should be given "if possible," he said that a request of 24 hours' notice from "a lot of hoodlums" meant nothing. Mr. Brown denied that he wished imprisonment of seamen, first proposing imprisonment "at the discretion of the Court," and then adding further:

> . . . and now I will say, on behalf of the Maritime Exchange of New York, that we are willing to accept, in lieu of imprisonment at the discretion of the Court, a provision granting to the master and officers of a vessel when the seaman deserts the authority and power to apprehend such deserting seaman wherever he may be found, and to take him back on board the vessel. . . .
>
> MR. FURUSETH: If we must have one of the two, we had rather take the humanity of the jail.
>
> MR. MINOR: Now why should the vessel owners have any more right to imprison men than these mill owners?
>
> MR. BROWN: In answer to that I will state a proposition which I think nobody will deny or seek to refute: That these seamen on board vessels of the United States are the wards of the nation; that they are men incapable of making a civil contract of the kind American citizens are capable of making. They are taken care of the same as orphans are. Special legislation stands on the statute books today to safeguard their interests and take care of them. . . . If special legislation is to be enacted to see that they do not abuse the privileges under which they live, the shipowner must be hedged about with some measure of protection.

Mr. Sharwood of the Philadelphia Exchange asserted the necessity of imprisonment from the owner's standpoint.

> MR. FURUSETH: [Does the Philadelphia Maritime Association claim] that imprisonment, or the threat of imprisonment, is necessary to keep them on their contract and on the vessel?

MR. SHARWOOD: Yes, we favor the imprisonment clause as necessary.

These views of the necessity of imprisonment for desertion, shared by owners and courts alike, are of particular interest in view of the fact that, after the abolition of that penalty in the coastwise trade, the number of desertions actually diminished.

Legislative Results

The committee reported out two bills embodying the main features of the Maguire bills, modified somewhat by compromise, and the chairman, Sereno E. Payne, introduced them as H.R. 2683 and H.R. 6399. The former, containing the least important provisions for the seamen, was enacted into law March 3, 1897. It made some improvement as to forecastle space, and dealt with the disposal of deceased seamen's wages and effects, and the offices of shipping commissioners and shipment and discharge in their presence. The other bill abolishing imprisonment for desertion from American vessels in ports of the United States regardless of the trade in which the vessel might be engaged, abolishing allotment and advance, and facilitating the punishment of brutal officers, passed the House. The Senate passed a substitute with amendments by Senator Frye which the seamen feared would open wide the door to legalized corporal punishment aboard ship by retaining the "justifiable cause" clause. The Sailors' Union sent a memorial to the Senate protesting against the substitute, and the session ended without the enactment of the seamen's main bill.

Arago Decision

After the passage of the Maguire Act, seamen generally believed that they could leave vessels in ports of the

United States when dissatisfied with their employment without fear of imprisonment. But the courts soon gave a somewhat different construction to the act. Four seamen, Robert Robertson, John Bradley, P. H. Olsen, and Morris Hanson shipped aboard the barkentine "Arago" at San Francisco in May, 1895, for a voyage to Knappton, Washington, thence to Chile, thence to such other foreign ports as the master might direct, and thence to return to the United States. But becoming dissatisfied with their employment, and believing they had the right under the Maguire Act to do so, they left the ship at Knappton and went to Astoria, Oregon. There they were arrested, taken before a justice of the peace, and committed to jail for some 16 days, until the "Arago" was ready to put to sea. Then against their will they were put on board by the United States Marshal. At sea they refused to obey the command of the master to "turn to." He thereupon put them in irons and brought them to San Francisco where they were arrested and put in the Alameda County jail. The case in the lower court was decided against the seamen, so, backed by the Sailors' Union, they appealed to the Supreme Court of the United States. The four seamen remained in jail nine months to hasten the hearing. On January 25, 1897, the Supreme Court, Justice Harlan dissenting, handed down what was to the seamen the "Second Dred Scott Decision." (*Robertson v. Baldwin*, 165 U. S. 275.)

The court held that although arrested in a coast port, the seamen had engaged for a foreign voyage, and therefore were not protected by the Maguire Act. It gave a lengthy opinion stating the nature of the thirteenth amendment, holding that the words "involuntary servitude" were intended to prevent the revival of slavery under a system like Mexican peonage or the Chinese coolie trade and did not apply to involuntary servitude wherever it existed. It cited the ancient law of the Rhodians, the *Consolato del Mare,* the *Judgments of Oleron,* and the *Laws of Wisbuy* to show that "from the oldest historical period the contract of the sailor has been treated as an exceptional one, involving, to a certain extent, the surrender of his personal liberty during the life of the contract." And referring to the act of 1790 the court said:

> In the face of this legislation upon the subject of desertion and absence without leave, which was in force in this country for more than sixty years before the Thirteenth Amendment was adopted, and similar legislation abroad from time immemorial it cannot be open to doubt that the provision against involuntary servitude was never intended to apply to their contracts. . . .
>
> Indeed the business of navigation could scarcely be carried on without some guaranty, beyond the ordinary civil remedies upon contract, that the sailor will not desert the ship at a critical moment, or leave her at some place where seamen are impossible to be obtained—as Molloy forcibly expresses it—"to rot in her neglected brine."

This case, while a severe shock to the seamen, only made them the more determined to change the law. They went back to the 55th Congress with their bill which had failed in the 54th Congress, and it was introduced in the Senate by Stephen M. White of California, and in the House by Judge Maguire. Upon the advice of Representative Payne, who had reported out their House bill the previous session, the seamen concentrated their efforts upon the Senate, endeavoring to get the Senate to enact a measure in which the House Committee, of which Payne was chairman, could recommend concurrence with such amendments as might be necessary to preserve its original intent.

The Seamen's Friends

This time the welfare societies rendered considerable aid in informing the public and Congress as to the condition of the sailor. Mr. J. K. Paulding of the Social Reform Club of New York went so far as to have a pamphlet entitled "What should be done for our sailors?" printed and distributed at his own expense. Rabbi K. Leonard Levy of Philadelphia appeared before the Senate Committee on Commerce in behalf of the bill. Even so, the attitude of most of their "friends" was not all the seamen felt that they had a right to expect. Though the joint conference of some seven welfare organizations of New York early in 1898 adopted and forwarded to Congress by personal representatives a resolution on the whole favorable to seamen, they still expressed preference for certain features of the Frye bill No. 623 over the seamen's bill, namely, the reduction of allotments to "original creditors" in the foreign trade to one month's wages, and imprisonment at the discretion of the court, instead of the total abolition of both, for which the seamen were fighting. The seamen were grateful for their assistance as far as it went, but felt keenly that it should have gone further.

The war with Spain, which broke out while the bill was under consideration, caused its temporary postponement to give preference to a rush of war legislation. But the net result seems to have been, as Andrew Furuseth reported, a general realization of the need for better laws for sailors "when the difficulty of obtaining a sufficient number of seamen qualified for the navy made it manifest that the navigation law and the general condition of seamen is such as to discourage American boys, who might, under more favorable conditions, seek the sea for a living."

In addition to those already mentioned, Samuel Gompers, George Chance, J. A. Rosendale of Philadelphia, J. Augustus Johnson of New York, and Andrew Furuseth appeared before the Committee on Commerce in support of the bill.

The bill was sent to the subcommittee on shipping, which amended it by striking out the provisions for watch and watch, and for larger forecastles, and by inserting allotment in the foreign trade not to exceed one month's wages and one month's imprisonment for desertion in a foreign port at the discretion of the judge.   In that form the bill passed the Senate on July 2, but the closing of the session prevented action by the House.

The White Act

Early in the next session the bill was taken up by the House.   The seamen, fearing to endanger the passage of the bill by insisting on amendments including all their demands, were content to see it pass on December 13, 1898, in the form in which it came from the Senate.   On December 21 the President signed the bill, known as the White Act, and it became law.   As passed, its principal features were: abolition of imprisonment for desertion from American vessels in any port of the United States; reduction from three to one month's imprisonment for desertion in a foreign port, and then only at the discretion of the judge; one month's wage permitted as allotment to an "original creditor" in the foreign trade; total abolition of corporal punishment, and a provision binding the master to surrender to justice subordinates guilty of the infliction of corporal punishment; the majority of the crew, without concurrence of an officer as previously required, given the right to demand the survey of an unseaworthy vessel before commencement of the voyage; and an improved scale of rations.

It also gave seamen on vessels of the United States the right to receive in ports of loading and discharging cargo half of the wages due them, unless the contrary was expressly stipulated in the contract. The previous proportion (fixed by the act of July 20, 1790) had been one-third wages due, with a like proviso. In both cases the proviso was the means of rendering the right of no practical value. It became important only with the abolition of the proviso in 1915.

Regarded from the point of view of immediate economic success, the years 1893–1898 were a complete failure, but the union had justified its existence many times over during these same years by what it did for the permanent improvement of the seamen. Through its activities the Maguire and White acts were passed. The "Red Record" was published, acquainting the public with the prevalence of brutality aboard American deep-water vessels, and assisting in its abolition in law and fact. The case of the "Arago" sailors, forced to serve against their will, was carried to the Supreme Court of the United States, and when the final decision went against them, the union changed the law by securing the passage of the White Act.

Unions and Law Enforcement

But laws do not enforce themselves. The need for labor organizations is not past when model legislation is placed upon the statute books. Of the truth of this statement there is abundant proof in the records of the Sailors' Union, which show the enforcement of the laws relating to seamen to be one of the most constant of the union's activities. During this period of the nineties the records are full of accounts of union efforts to enforce the laws, particularly against advance and crimping. The importance of an organization to enforce laws benefiting its members is most forcibly illustrated by the effectiveness of the new legal prohibitions of advance and allotment secured and backed by a vigilant union. In marked contrast was the failure of the act of 1884, nullified and then repealed because of the power of crimps when no union to compel its enforcement existed. During these years, as indeed throughout its existence, the union assisted many a seaman to secure his rights under the law, and bore the financial burden of carrying through the higher courts cases involving points of legal interpretation vital to all seamen.

Thus ended the second phase of the legal struggle of the seamen for freedom. During years of business depression the union had turned, as labor has turned so often, from the economic to the political field. The rewards of this policy were great. American seamen in American ports were free men, as free to give or withhold their personal services as men ashore. The longer and more tedious but no less important task now remained to work for the extension of this freedom to seamen of all nations in all ports of the world.

CHAPTER VII

COLLECTIVE BARGAINING[1]

Union Successes with Business Prosperity

With the return of business prosperity and shipping activity the efforts of the union in the industrial field began to attain some measure of success. In the spring of 1899 the sailors struck successfully against the Shipowners' Association, composed at this time of owners of sailing vessels. The strike was called to secure a $5 raise in the Mexican trade. The waterfront was picketed, and after three months the owners were all paying the union wage.

For a long time the union had lost all control over the shipping in the steamers. Many of the men sailing in them were old union men whom economic necessity had compelled to "scab" when the strikes persistently went against the union, and who now opposed reimposition of union control because that meant they would be compelled to pay up all their back dues.

Following the successful strike in the sailing vessels a campaign was undertaken to unionize the steamers again by remitting all but $9 of back dues to former

---

[1]Sources for this chapter are:
Minutes of the Sailors' Union (see page 64).
International Longshoremen's Association. Annual Convention Proceedings of the Pacific District.
International Seamen's Union of America. Annual Convention Proceedings. Constitution and By-Laws, 1917.
American Federation of Labor. Proceedings. Bloomington, Illinois, and Washington, 1881——.
Blum, Solomon. Jurisdictional Disputes Resulting from Structural Differences in American Trade Unions. Berkeley, 1913.
Jensen, George C. The City Front Federation of San Francisco. Berkeley, 1912 (MS).
Files of San Francisco newspapers.

union men.   As a result the membership grew rapidly.
"Nothing succeeds like success."   The ability of the union
to enforce its demands against the shipowners made it
plain to sailors that belonging to the organization was
worth while.   The membership in good standing grew
in the two years after the strike of 1899 from 1,288 to
3,465.

Seamen and Longshoremen Again

In September and October, 1900, there was further
trouble with the longshoremen.   The latter, in a secret
agreement, secured the consent of the Teamsters' Union
to refuse to deliver cargo destined for the Hawaiian
Islands to anyone except longshoremen, thus boycotting
vessels until the seamen were discharged.   The seamen
were thereupon promptly discharged and the longshoremen got the work.   When the seamen explained the
situation to the teamsters, the latter readily revised their
agreement with the longshoremen, and agreed to handle
the freight regardless of who loaded it upon the vessels.
To settle the trouble with the longshoremen, the sailors
entered into an agreement with them whereby seamen
were to work only inside the rail; each union was to
refuse to give or receive freight from non-union men,
and longshoremen were to recognize the right of a full
union crew to work cargo aboard ship.   For a time there
was peace between the two unions, but only for a time.

City Front Federation

At the beginning of the century, there was a great
boom in industrial activity in San Francisco, following
the war activities on the Pacific and the return of prosperity to the country at large.   Labor was scarce—it was
a good time to strike.   New unions rapidly sprang up

throughout the city to take advantage of the opportunity. To prevent labor from organizing, and to oppose the unions already in existence, an association of employers was formed, whose policy was to destroy the labor organizations one at a time. Many of the younger unions, hastily organized, struck rashly and were crushed. It was to control the policy of these weaker unions as well as to resist the Employers' Association directly that very early in 1901 the City Front Federation of waterfront unions was formed. The jealousies between the waterfront unions were as strong as ever, and only the grave common danger forced them to unite. Although the strikes were taking place uptown, their results were beginning to be felt in shipping, and the sailors realized that they were likely to be drawn in at any time.

Strike of 1901

In the third week in July, 1901, the teamsters refused, in accordance with their interpretation of their agreement with their employers, to deliver certain goods. Behind this immediate cause, however, lay the real cause, fear of the Employers' Association. The City Front Federation, of which body they were members, voted a strike resolution in support of the teamsters, and the Sailors' Union as well as the other affiliated unions, approved. In the eyes of the unions it was a case of all standing together, or waiting to be destroyed singly. From the employer's standpoint, the issue involved was the right to manage his own business without outside interference. To the employee the issue was the right to unionize. One view was but the obverse of the other. To each side the issue was plain.

The entire City Front Federation went out. Some 12,000 struck, only about 1,100 remaining at work.

About 65 per cent of the regular business was stopped, according to labor estimates. The seamen at once took steps actively to prosecute the strike. Watches of pickets were established on the waterfront. An executive committee was chosen to take charge of the situation, and empowered to board men who were out of employment on account of the strike; $1,000 was donated to the longshoremen to support them during the strike. Throughout August efforts were made to negotiate with the Employers' Association, but without success. Pickets were clubbed by the police and arrested wholesale, but the union maintained the watches, cautioning pickets against violence, and advising them to keep out of the way of the police. In the latter part of September the Oakland teamsters were advised by the federation to go back on terms maintaining the *status quo ante,* and the strike in Oakland was accordingly called off. On October 2 after negotiations with the employers, the City Front Federation declared the entire strike off.

The struggle had lasted for two and one-half months and ended in a draw, the employers promising not to discriminate against union men. It has been stated that the strike was broken by the influx of agricultural workers, the importation of negroes by the Employers' Association, and the assistance of students from the University of California. That these factors did work serious harm to the union cause is undoubted, but there is no evidence that the employers gained any advantage over either the seamen or the other workers as a result of the strike.

Negotiation with Shipowners

Nevertheless, the union was by no means overconfident. Many whalers, Alaska fishermen, gold-seekers from Nome, and Chileans were ashore as non-union men.

So when the reorganized Shipowners' Association, with James Rolph as president, proposed certain terms to the union, the men felt it best to accept them, even though they were not wholly satisfactory, and to use the ensuing period of peace to organize all San Francisco and the Bay region.

Negotiations over controverted points lasted five months. The union refused a sliding scale of wages based upon freights. Its contention on this point was that freights are beyond the sailors' control. Further, it was argued that since many of the steam schooner managers were also lumber merchants and owners of mill and forest, it was to their interest to keep freights down while the price of lumber rose, so as to avoid having to divide the increase in freight with the other shareholders of the vessel. The seamen also argued that wages form but a small percentage of operating costs, and that when all pay the same wages the particular rate of wages is of no concern to owners since they are all on the same competitive footing. The union also objected to declaring against sympathetic strikes, opposed the establishment of a shipowners' shipping office, and insisted on a 9-hour day as the basis for overtime as against a 54-hour week basis. Finally a compromise was reached, and on April 3, 1902, the union signed its first formal working and wages agreement with the Shipowners' Association.

Full Recognition of Union

The union had now, after seventeen years of struggle, won full recognition from the shipowners. This marked the beginning of a period in which wages and conditions for seamen were determined by joint negotiations, with the results embodied in formal collective agreements.

The details of the first agreement are worthy of note, for they show the conditions under which the seamen worked at that time. The agreement was to be in force for a period of six months and thereafter until 30 days' notice of abrogation, in writing, by either party. The principal points agreed upon were:

1. Wages were to be $45 for sailing vessels to outside ports, $40 for inside ports, $35 to the Islands and Mexico, and $30 to South America, China, Japan, and Australia.
2. The Shipowners' Association was to maintain a shipping office in San Francisco but no shipping master (crimp).
3. Outside of San Francisco, agents of the Sailors' Union were to furnish crews.
4. A 9-hour day was recognized, and overtime.
5. The Sailors' Union declared itself opposed to the policy of sympathetic strikes.
6. A standing committee was provided to adjust grievances.

The policy of entering into similar agreements with the Shipowners' Association has been followed continuously down to the strike of May, 1921. About a year after this first agreement with the Shipowners' Association, a similar one was entered into with the Steam Schooner Managers' Association.

At that time the coasting sailing vessel owners were organized into the Shipowners' Association of the Pacific Coast, which incorporated in 1904, but which had been in existence long before. The steam schooner owners and managers were also united in a loose organization called the Steam Schooner Managers' (or Owners') Association. In the latter part of 1906 the two organizations were merged under the name of the Shipowners' Association.

This organization still exists, and in 1923 had 45 members with 127 steam and sailing vessels and motorships entered in the association.

Enforcement of Agreements

With most of the coast shipping now covered by agreements, the chief routine business of the union naturally settled itself into enforcing the terms of the agreements. On the one hand there was continual necessity for the interpretation of the working rules when applied to actual cases over which a difficulty arose; and on the other, the union found its own members giving trouble by signing on and then at the last minute refusing to sail. This situation was not new. As early as 1897 it had been used against the seamen, when Senator Frye of Maine, arguing in favor of retaining imprisonment for desertion, said:

> Sailors desert when first shipment is made rather than during the voyage, thus causing large demurrage expense to the vessel, and no loss to seamen for they have earned no wages to forfeit.

The union recognized the harm it suffered through such actions of its members and exerted all possible moral pressure to check them. In 1907 stringent disciplinary measures were taken. During that year, of 128 members fined by the union, most of them were convicted of backing out at the last moment.

Jurisdictional Dispute with Longshoremen

The slumbering rivalry between the seamen and the longshoremen broke out afresh in 1902. The agreement of 1900 had brought peace on the Pacific coast; but when, without any warning, the longshoremen's convention changed the name of their organization from "International Longshoremen's Association" to "International

Longshoremen, Marine, and Transport Workers' Association," the seamen became alarmed. They felt that the longshoremen were trying to bring seamen within the longshore organization so that the jurisdiction of the longshore organization might be extended at the expense of the seamen's unions, and the cargo work of the seamen further encroached upon by the longshoremen. If the change were allowed to stand, it meant ultimately either that the International Seamen's Union must become a branch of the International Longshoremen, Marine, and Transport Workers' Association, or that the seamen's union would be merged into the local longshore unions.

The trouble grew out of the situation in the Great Lakes where the Marine Firemen, Oilers and Watertenders had affiliated in 1899 with the longshoremen there. The longshoremen laid no claim to deck sailors, but did claim firemen, oilers, watertenders, engineers, masters, pilots, licensed tugmen, etc. The seamen, on the other hand, claimed the line of demarcation to be "the line that separates the vessel from the dock—in other words, the line between land and water," and asserted their jurisdiction over "all unions whose members make living by following the sea, lake, or river in any capacity in steam or sailing vessels." The seamen recognized, however, that licensed officers are not "trade unionists in the accepted sense," but wished to be on friendly and mutually helpful terms with them.

Here were two organizations, formed on industrial lines, fighting over jurisdiction, the one fearing absorption by the other. Strangely enough, the seamen's delegates stressed "trade autonomy" and "craft," while both the International Seamen's Union and the longshoremen were organized on lines of industrial federation. This was probably because craft autonomy was a shibboleth among most of the American Federation of Labor, and could be appealed to with great effect, rather than because of any failure to recognize the fact that both contending parties were federations of craft unions grouped on industrial lines. The seamen carried their fight through several conventions of the American Federation of Labor, finally compelling the longshoremen to drop the objectionable title and resume their original name of "International Longshoremen's Association."

Sailors vs. Longshoremen on Pacific

On the Pacific coast the struggle was bitterly fought out between the Sailors' Union and the longshoremen, especially in Portland and Puget Sound ports. The San Francisco longshoremen withdrew from their own International when the inclusive title continued to be the object of strife, and sided with the sailors. But the Portland and Puget Sound longshoremen refused to load vessels along with the sailors in the offshore trade, charging that the sailors too frequently loaded on coasting sailors' pay, which was lower than longshoremen's, and then let a new crew take the vessel to sea on wages which were still lower. The sailors thereupon did all the loading. A fight followed. The longshoremen announced their readiness to furnish non-union crews to masters free of charge, and worked hand in hand with the crimps against the union sailors. The sailors sought and received the aid of the shipowners. The struggle went on for several months, until by August, 1905, the sailors forced the longshoremen to give up their claims.

Gompers' Award

In 1907, Samuel Gompers, to whom the matter had been referred as arbitrator, handed down his decision that the use of the additional title "Marine and Transport Workers" should be discontinued. The longshoremen's convention at first refused to abide by the award, but a later convention was persuaded to accede. The remainder of Gompers' decision provided:

The work of loading and unloading vessels (with the following exceptions) belongs to the longshoremen:

(a) In the coastwise trade, when seamen bring a vessel into port, remain with the vessel for its onward course or for its return to the initial port, the work of loading or unloading the cargo at the extent of the ship's tackle may be performed by the seamen.

(b) Seamen may load or unload cargoes, beyond the ship's tackle, but only with the consent of or by agreement with the longshoremen. .

3. Under no circumstances (unless by the consent of or agreement with the longshoremen) may seamen load or unload cargoes unless they (the seamen) are of the vessel's sailing crew in an in- or out-bound voyage. And then only as above described.

This decision did not specifically mention cargo work on vessels in the offshore trade. The omission gave rise to further trouble on the Pacific northwest coast in 1912 and 1913. The difficulty started when members of the Sailors' Union again loaded vessels in the foreign trade at sailors' pay, and then quit the vessel, allowing it to proceed with a crew paid at deep-water rates and sometimes a non-union crew besides. This action amounted to undercutting the rates for longshore work. Consequently the longshoremen passed a resolution refusing to work with the crew of vessels in the foreign trade, thus reopening the controversy of 1905. Further, a *dual* union of longshoremen supported by the employers was organized in Portland and many of the sailors joined. The difficulty was at last amicably settled, however, by the sailors' and longshoremen's representatives at a convention in Seattle.

Cargo Work on Vessels

The work of loading and discharging cargo on the Pacific coast is now carried on in accordance with the Gompers decision. In the coastwise lumber trade (and in very small vessels of the offshore trade) the sailors work cargo "from tackle to tackle." The crew handles all cargo work aboard ship, unless extra men are needed. These men can be taken from the longshoremen. The longshoremen handle all the cargo ashore. This means that such ships usually carry a slightly larger crew, and pay higher wages per man, but the arrangement is more economical and satisfactory to the owners than to pay the higher longshoremen's wages for all cargo work and to depend on being able to get longshoremen at all ports along the coast to commence the loading of lumber just as soon as the vessel arrives. In all other vessels the longshoremen on the Pacific coast customarily do all the cargo work aboard and on shore. On the Atlantic coast practically all cargo work on all vessels is done by longshoremen.

New Demands on Shipowners

In the spring of 1906 negotiations were entered into with the steam schooner owners, now called the San Francisco Steamship Association, for the renewal of their agreement. Disagreement arose over the sailors' demand for an increase in wages in steam schooners from $45 to $50. On the 16th of April the sailors voted for the second time to insist upon the increase. Two days later the great earthquake and fire occurred, devastating the city of San Francisco. On account of this disaster, the demand was postponed for several weeks until shipping was restored to normal, and the price of lumber and freights began to rise because of 'the great demand for materials for the rebuilding of the city.

The owners of sailing vessels then voluntarily increased wages from $40 to $45 to all open ports south of San Francisco; from $35 to $40 in the trade to the Hawaiian Islands; and from $30 to $35 to the Philippine Islands and Siberia. But the steam schooner owners refused to grant the $5 per month increase. The Steamship Association was at that time affiliated with the United Shipping and Transportation Association, which in turn was alleged to be the maritime branch of the Citizens' Alliance, an organization whose object was to establish the open shop. However that may be, the shipowners denied that the Citizens' Alliance had anything to do with the dispute between the sailors and steam schooner owners. When the renewed demand was presented, the United Shipping and Transportation Association seems to have been willing to grant a $2.50 increase, and even admitted its ability to pay the entire amount, at the same time denying that it ought to be paid. There was evidently a deeper issue than wages at stake. The sailors (and the firemen and cooks with them) believed themselves entitled to demand and receive the increase; the owners regarded the threatened strike as unwarranted "interference on the part of Andrew Furuseth of the Sailors' Union to dictate to them how they shall run their vessels." Taking such a position, it was but natural that the owners should refuse offers of arbitration.

Strike of 1906

Open hostilities began on June 6 when the owners locked out the longshoremen, who until then had had no concern in the dispute. The fight, however, soon centered on the seamen, whereupon the seamen's unions voluntarily withdrew from the City Front Federation in order to remove all cause for locking out shore members of the federation. This action demonstrated to the employers the futility of trying to bring pressure to bear on the seamen through the City Front Federation, and the lockout was accordingly ended. The longshoremen of San Francisco and Eureka decided to load and unload vessels regardless of the union affiliation or non-affiliation of the crew. The San Pedro longshoremen, however, refused to do the seamen's work in loading and unloading, and as a result were locked out. This aid was acknowledged by the Sailors' Union at the close of the strike by a donation of $500.

The United Shipping and Transportation Association made efforts to force the independent steam schooners and the sailing vessels, which were organized into the Shipowners' Association of the Pacific Coast, either to take non-union crews or to lay up until the end of the strike. Pressure was brought to bear on the lumber mills, many of which were owned by members of the Steamship Association, to the end that the refractory vessels might find no lumber to transport. This policy was only partially successful with the independent steam schooner operators. The Shipowners' Association, whose sailing vessels were enjoying the best times in years, not only refused to join the United Shipping and Transportation Association, but on August 31 granted $5 increase in coasting wages, and a raise in overtime of from 40 to 50 cents an hour.

The strike, as usual, was marked by frequent violence. The owners endeavored to provide non-union crews from Mexicans, Japanese, and Hawaiians, and men and boys from inland. Private armed guards were placed aboard some of the vessels to keep off sailors, who, according to their accustomed tactics, came alongside to take off non-union crews which could be induced to leave. Upon more than one occasion these guards fired upon sailor pickets. From the steam schooner "National City" they used their weapons with such deadly effect that one sailor, Andrew Kellner, was killed outright, and three others were wounded, as their launch was drawing alongside. The employers also used the injunction to prohibit the union from interfering with non-union crews and vessels. The strike dragged on for five months, until, on October 31, the employers gave up the attempt to operate with non-union crews, granted the $5 increase, and signed an agreement with the union. Brisk shipping conditions were on the side of the men, and they won their struggle, notwithstanding the severe tactics which had been employed against them. But the price of victory, to the union treasury alone, was $25,000.

The years following the strike of 1906 were, in the main, years of prosperity for business and shipping. From 1906 to 1921 no strikes occurred on the Pacific coast (except in British Columbia). The union used the intervening period to build up its membership to include practically all seamen on the coast, to strengthen its power over all vessels, and to secure favorable legislation. The owners' lament that "the shipowner on this coast is now completely at the mercy of the Sailors' Union," and the passage of the Seamen's Act by Congress, are trustworthy evidence of the economic power and political successes of the union at this period.

Until 1916 little effort was made to raise wages. From 1908 the scale stood at $30 per month going offshore, $45 in sailing vessels on the coast; $50 in coasting steam vessels to inside ports, and $55 to open ports.

Fifty cents an hour was paid for overtime, with nine hours as the basic working day.

Sailors and Longshoremen

The records of the Sailors' Union during this period refer frequently to relations with the longshoremen. Sometimes it was a case of aid to the longshoremen through the sailors' refusal to discharge cargo to non-union longshoremen. At other times the longshoremen refused to load steamers carrying non-union crews. But mainly the references to longshoremen voice the protests of the sailors, fearing encroachments upon their share of the loading and unloading of cargo; or they reiterate the warnings of the watchful officers of the union lest the members, through carelessness in leaving the vessel before unloading, or through inadvertence, allow their work "to quietly pass into the hands of the longshoremen." In 1914 the longshoremen aroused the resentment of the sailors when one of the longshoremen's district councils sent a protest to Congress against the passage of the Seamen's bill, stating that under the proposed law large numbers of desertions would occur from foreign steamers touching in American ports, flooding the waterfronts with stranded foreign seamen who would be a menace to American longshoremen.

In 1916 the San Francisco longshoremen went out on strike, demanding a 35 per cent increase in wages, and asked the sailors to come out with them. The sailors refused, giving as reasons that the longshoremen in this case had broken their agreement with the owners by allowing practically no time for negotiation, and that they had failed to co-operate with the other waterfront unions through the Waterfront Federation. Furthermore, the longshoremen refused clearly to "recognize the seamen's first right to work in the vessel's cargo," in unequivocal terms; nor was the Sailors' Union willing to go on strike at the call of another organization. When the longshoremen struck again in 1919 the sailors took no cognizance of the controversy other than to declare their policy of performing their usual cargo work regardless of the union affiliation or non-affiliation of the longshoremen. And when the Waterfront Federation called a strike against the Charles Nelson Company to compel the employment of union longshoremen, the sailors maintained their policy of aloofness by promptly withdrawing from the Waterfront Federation.

CHAPTER VIII

THE SEAMEN'S ACT[1]

Legislative Efforts Renewed

The early legislative successes of the seamen had come rapidly. Furuseth's first journey to Washington in the interests of seamen's legislation in 1894 had been followed by the enactment of the Maguire Act the next year. Only three years later the White Act was passed, extending the effects of the previous law and bringing the seamen's goal a step nearer. So far as concerns American seamen alone, these acts are in some respects the most important victories the sailors have ever gained. But many legal changes full of import to domestic seamen were still necessary to complete the union program, and it yet remained to realize the goal of freedom for seamen of all nations. To the accomplishment of these aims the union leaders now bent their energies. But progress was very slow.

The years from 1898 to 1904 were spent chiefly in preparation and in the more perfect formulation of the draft of the seamen's bill by the International Seamen's Union legislative committee. In the meantime ship subsidy bills were opposed in 1899 and later in 1906. In 1904, Senator Alger of Michigan introduced a bill directed

---

[1] Sources for this chapter, in addition to interviews with shipping men and seamen are:
  Congressional Committee Hearings.
  Congressional Record. Containing the Proceedings and Debates, Washington, 1873——.
  Reports of Commissioner of Navigation.
  United States Bureau of Immigration. Annual Reports of the Commissioner General, Washington, 1892——.
  United States Shipping Board. Report of the Director of the Marine and Dock Industrial Relations Division. Washington, 1919.
  Pacific Marine Review. Seattle, San Francisco, 1904——.
  Legal Aid Society [of New York]. Annual Reports, New York.
  Proceedings of the International Seamen's Union (see page 94).

against the crimps which made the holding of sailors'
clothing a misdemeanor. This strengthening amendment
of the Maguire Act had the support of the Seamen's
Union and became law.

But with their main issues, the seamen were unable to
make much headway. In March, 1904, they were finally
able to get a hearing for their bill. Representative Liver-
nash, of California, introduced the measure as H. R.
13771. It was submitted to the Merchant Marine Commission of 1904, and testimony given in its behalf. But
the Commission, in its report, dismissed the case of the
seamen by "commend [-ing it] to the friendly attention
of the proper committees of the Senate and House of
Representatives," and proceeded to recommend to Congress a subsidy bill coupled with a naval reserve of merchant seamen. This subsidy bill the seamen bitterly
opposed on the ground that it "makes industrial employment contingent upon enlistment in the navy during the
seamen's entire military age," and for other reasons which
are given in detail in Chapter X.

Legislative History of La Follette Act

In the 60th and 61st Congresses Representative Spight,
of Mississippi, introduced the seamen's bill in the House
and in the 61st Congress, 2d session, Senator La Follette,
of Wisconsin, whom Furuseth had interested in his cause,
introduced the same bill in the Senate. This time hearings
on the bill were held by the House Committee on Merchant Marine and Fisheries, but it was not reported out of
the Committee. The following Congress the bill was
reintroduced by La Follette, and by William B. Wilson,
of Pennsylvania. The Wilson Bill was reported back from
the subcommittee on Navigation of the Committee on Merchant Marine and Fisheries at the close of the hearings in

January, 1912, and reported to the House on May 2, 1912. After a long debate it passed the House with some amendments. On the vote, which was without roll call, only three members were heard to vote in the negative. The Senate, after debate, likewise passed the bill, but with an amendment in which the House later concurred. The bill was presented to President Taft on March 4, 1913, the day on which he left office. Taft would not sign the eleventh-hour bill, so the seamen's leaders were forced to renew the fight the following session.

Senator Nelson, of Minnesota, reintroduced a bill to abolish imprisonment for desertion recommended by the Department of Commerce and Labor, which had also passed the Senate the previous session but which was not the seamen's bill. Senator La Follette then introduced the seamen's own bill as a substitute, striking out all except the enacting clause of the Nelson bill. After a vigorous debate this bill passed the Senate, went to the House where it was passed with an amendment, went to conference, and was finally passed by both Houses. On March 4, 1915, the Seamen's Act was signed by President Wilson, and went into effect six months later.

So much for a brief legislative history of the act which, according to its advocate, ushered in "The Dawn of the New Day" for the seamen, and according to its opponents, "the only effect of which is to drive the last American ship from the ocean."

In the following summary and analysis no attempt is made to include every provision of the act. Likewise no endeavor is made to follow all the ramifications of the arguments pro and con, but rather to indicate the positions of seamen and shipowners in their main outlines, with especial attention to the reasons for the positions taken. This brevity of statement is not intended to minimize the weight or importance of the arguments and provisions omitted. Their inclusion, however, does not seem necessary to an understanding of the seamen's movement as it found expression in the passage of the Seamen's Act.

Summary of the Seamen's Act

The Seamen's Act is entitled "An Act to promote the welfare of American seamen in the merchant marine of the United States: to abolish arrest and imprisonment as a penalty for desertion and to secure the abrogation of treaty provisions in relation thereto; and to promote safety at sea." Argument for the bill was developed along the three lines indicated in the title, and it was on these grounds that the seamen finally succeeded in securing the passage of their measure. Some of the provisions of the act, in brief summary and analysis, are as follows:

1. Imprisonment for Desertion Abolished

To abolish arrest and imprisonment as a penalty for desertion, the act in effect extended the freedom for which seamen had previously contended and had secured for American seamen in ports of the United States through the Maguire and White Acts by providing:

(a) Forfeiture of personal effects left on board and wages earned as the only penalty for desertion in safe harbor.

(b) Abrogation of all treaties providing for the arrest and return of deserters from foreign vessels.

(c) The right to demand half of wages earned and unpaid in ports of loading or discharging cargo, all stipulations in the contract to the contrary notwithstanding, this to apply to foreign seamen in American ports as well as to seamen on American vessels in all ports.

Arguments Pro and Con

The abolition of arrest and imprisonment for desertion has always been in the forefront of the demands of the seamen. They have sought it in the name of the abolition of "serfdom" and involuntary servitude, and have appealed for it on the plea that they alone were not free men. This was scoffed at by the shipowners, whose opinion of the passage of the Seamen's Act was expressed as follows:

> It was won by continual fighting along the lines of appeal to the heart rather than to the brain . . . the "terrible slavery" of the poor, downtrodden sailor had become an obsession with many men at Washington.

The right to receive half of the wages due in foreign ports, the seamen argued, would reduce desertions, by rendering the sailor less dependent on crimps and boarding masters when he went ashore, and so less likely to be enticed or cajoled into deserting. The shipowners protested on the grounds that the men would go ashore, get drunk, forget to come back on time and delay the vessel, or that they would get half of their wages in a foreign port where seamen were scarce, threaten to desert, and thus unfairly force the master to raise their wages. In the case of the extension to foreign sailors of the right of American seamen to receive half-wages, and to be free from fear of imprisonment for desertion, the seamen argued that the foreign seamen coming to American ports would, by desertion or the threat of desertion, compel the master to raise their wages to, or nearly to, the American level, thus tending to equalize American and foreign seamen's wages to the advantage of the American shipowners. This argument, however, failed to win over the shipowners to support of the bill in Congress.

2. Welfare Provisions

To promote the welfare of American seamen, to create such conditions as would bring back the native American to the sea, and thus build up American sea power, the act provided:

> (a) An increase in the forecastle space for each man from 72 to 120 cubic feet with additional provision for hospital space and washrooms.

During the hearings on the bill, Andrew Furuseth built a canvas forecastle the exact size of a sailor's allotted space, and exhibited it in the committee rooms to convince the legislators of the justice of his demand for more space.

> (b) An increase in the daily food scale of an ounce of butter and a quart of water.

This provision was of practical importance in some classes of vessels, mainly sailing ships in the offshore trade. Crews are now generally fed better than the law requires.

> (c) The vessel or owner, as well as the master, made liable for failure to surrender an officer guilty of inflicting corporal punishment on members of the crew, if such officer escape.
> (d) Total abolition of allotment to an "original creditor" (extended to foreign as well as American ports in 1920), in an effort to break further the hold of the crimps.
> (e) A 9-hour day in port.

These provisions were not severely contested. The owners, however, scoffed at provisions for the welfare of "American" seamen, because a majority of our sailors are foreign born.

3. Safety Measures

In the interest of safety at sea, the act provided:

(a) A scale of manning for passenger vessels based upon the number of lifeboats carried, and prohibited passenger vessels on ocean routes more than 20 nautical miles offshore from carrying more passengers than can be accommodated in the lifeboats and pontoon life rafts.

(b) 65 per cent of the deck crew of all vessels must be able seamen.

(c) 75 per cent of the crew in each department of the vessel must be able to understand any order given by the officers.

(d) The majority of the crew, independently of the officers, was given the right to demand a survey in foreign ports to determine the seaworthiness of a vessel. According to the White Act this right could be exercised only prior to the commencement of the voyage.

(e) Division of the deck crew into two watches, and of the firemen, oilers, and watertenders into three watches, for the purpose of preventing undermanning and overwork. When this section is not complied with, the seaman is entitled to discharge and to receive wages earned.

Pro and Con

On each point the owners took issue with the seamen, holding the provisions to be unnecessary to safety and unduly burdensome to shipping. However, the wave of public opinion which swept over the world following the Titanic disaster aided the seamen to carry this point. We will not attempt in this book to deal with the merits of means taken to increase safety at sea; we are dealing here only with the interests involved in the controversy.

The fight centered chiefly over the language clause and

the able seaman requirement. The seamen, by means of the language clause, wanted to drive the Asiatics from American vessels on the Pacific. The owners openly defended the seamanship of Orientals, and held that to be denied the right to employ them in the trans-Pacific trade the same as their competitors, would drive their ships from American registry. From the sailor's point of view, the purpose of the able seaman clause was to protect him against influx of the unskilled into his craft—which had become possible through the displacement of sail by steam—not only in normal times but also during strikes. The owners opposed such restrictions on their employment of men both on grounds of higher manning costs, and on the helpless position in which they would be left during strikes.

In the seamen's strike on this coast, several years ago, the commercial lines worried along for a considerable period using office men and other landsmen whose services could be obtained, to take the places of the seamen, waiters and others and operated successfully although the continued harassing tactics of the union made operations necessarily expensive and the lines involved eventually surrendered to the union. When this law becomes effective, if it does, it will in the future be a case of surrender without a fight because landsmen cannot be used to perform such services even though they can properly do so, when instructed in the duties, because they have not served one or more years at sea (E. F. Grandpré, in *Pacific Marine Review,* September, 1915).

So much for a brief review of the more important provisions of the Seaman's Act and the main arguments of seamen and shipowners.

This is the act for which Andrew Furuseth, backed by the organized seamen of America, spent twenty-one years in Washington. He worked for it continuously from 1894, winning a victory in 1895, another in 1898, and the final triumph in 1915. What, then, is the significance of the sections of this act for which the American seamen's movement, led from the Pacific, has fought, why the persistent demand for freedom, for the abolition of the "serfdom" of the sailor?

Economic Significance of Freedom

The truth of the matter is that freedom is not the end; it is the means. The Seamen's Act is not the goal, but the weapon. It "is not a roasted goose, it is a gun with which to shoot the goose." The purpose achieved through the increase of the sailors' personal freedom is this: to enable the sailors to fight their economic battles equipped with the same legal right to quit work that free men ashore possess.

"Working the Oracle"

Let Furuseth explain this tactical significance of freedom by which the condition of the craft is to be improved:

The vessel is ready and the master orders the lines cast off. You cast your duds on the wharf and then follow the duds. The vessel is delayed. She must find another crew. This crew may do the same thing or go up the coast and leave her there. She is is again delayed. How long will the shipowners stand for that, especially in passenger vessels.

We did this years ago. . . . We did it when the owners and the boarding masters were together. We did it even when we were arrested for it and were brought back to the vessel and compelled to work.

We certainly can do it now when we cannot be arrested for doing it in any safe harbor. The seamen's law, Section 7, gives all seamen in American ports the right to quit work at will. You will lose what money you have coming to you, that is true. What are you willing to do to get rid of the shipowners' office here and elsewhere? If you are not willing to do that much you will never get rid of those shipping offices.

Next we are told the reasons for the particular way in which sections of the Seamen's Act were drawn:

You need not lose the money, however, because Section 2 of the Seamen's Act provides that you shall be divided into at least two watches, to be on deck alternately or successively. It further says that when this is not done (where day men are carried) the contract is broken, and you are entitled to your discharge and the money you have earned. . . . When they begin to keep the law about the watches and you cannot get your money in that way, we have another section of the Seamen's Act which gives you one-half of the wages due to you in any port (not oftener than after each fifth day)—this Section 4. Of course, you will lose some of your wages now and then in this fight, but if you are not willing to do this, then you prefer serfdom to freedom, then for you there is no help. God himself cannot help the man who will not help himself. Are you willing to help yourself? If you are, study this and learn how to use it. . . .

The economic significance of the Seamen's Act to the American seaman is clear. He has labored under the disability of a legal status which was not that of a free man, and which handicapped him in his efforts to raise the economic and social position of his calling. Therefore he demanded and received, in the Seamen's Act, the same freedom, and a recognition of the same right to quit work, as belongs to free men ashore. He has felt the competition of the Oriental and the unskilled. Therefore he asked for the language clause and for experience requirements in the rating of seamen.

Further, the low wages of foreign seamen have curtailed the employment of American seamen in the foreign trade and have kept American wages from rising to a higher level. Laborers ashore are free to sell their labor in the highest market. But shipowners ship men in the lowest market for a round voyage. The Seamen's Act, giving the right to quit and to demand half of wages earned, is intended to force all shipowners, equally, to ship men in the highest labor market, and thus level wages of seamen upward instead of keeping them down. If that be accomplished, the low wages of foreign competitors will no longer stand in the way of higher wages and the more extensive employment of American seamen on American ships.

These provisions were included in the La Follette Act by the seamen's leaders for the benefit of seamen. They were argued for, and finally passed after twenty-one years' consideration on the ground that they were in accordance with sound public policy.

Operation of the Seamen's Act

The Seamen's Act was signed March 4, 1915. In spite of a flood of adverse press criticism launched against it between March and November, it went into effect in the latter month as regards American vessels. By July, 1916, it had gone into effect as respects vessels of other countries, the treaties concerning the arrest and imprisonment of deserters having been abrogated in accordance with the law. The abnormal conditions caused by the war complicate any effort at analysis of the operation of the Seamen's Act. Nevertheless, some conclusions can be drawn as to its workings in the brief and disturbed years during which it has been in effect.

The Language Test

Both seamen and shipowners agree that the language test has never been enforced to the extent of preventing employment of Chinese crews on American vessels. The seamen's only other hope of achieving this purpose lies in the raising of Oriental seamen's wages, making the employment of American sailors on American ships equally profitable with the employment of Orientals. To bring this about, complete equalization of wages would be unnecessary, for ships with Oriental crews carry a much larger number of sailors because of the difference in efficiency. During the war it was impossible to enforce the 65 per cent able seamen clause because of the enormous increase in our merchant marine. This dilution of labor during the war, however, was agreed to by the seamen's unions. Other sections of the law, such as the forecastle space provision, and provisions as to payment of wages earned, have been more strictly carried out.

Shipowners have complained of the evils of the half-wage clause, which they allege gives the seamen money to keep them drunk while ashore, renders them inefficient when they return to the vessel, and at times causes delay in sailing. This complaint is supported by considerable consular authority, and, considered by itself, is a legitimate grievance. But since such complaints were made long before the Seamen's Act it seems unjustifiable to lay the entire blame at the door of this law.

No epidemic of desertion by American seamen leaving our vessels stranded in foreign ports has followed the abolition of imprisonment for quitting the vessel in safe harbor, although such instances have occurred. And failure to join the vessel after signing articles, for which there has been virtually no penalty since the Maguire and White Acts, remains a negligible factor, amounting, in the case of men shipped before a shipping commissioner, to less than 2 per cent.

Effect on Merchant Marine

Whether or not the Seamen's Act has driven the American merchant from the Pacific is a disputed question. The withdrawal of the Pacific Mail Steamship Company, shipowners maintained, was due to the act. They say the practical non-existence of privately owned cargo carriers in the trans-Pacific trade at the present time (1923) is proof of the fact that the Seamen's Act, although not the only legislative handicap to American shipping, is the culmination of the hampering policy long followed by Congress. As to the withdrawal of the Pacific Mail, the testimony of R. P. Schwerin, vice-president and manager of the Pacific Mail, given in 1912 and 1913, before congressional committees, casts much doubt on the statement that the Seamen's Act caused the withdrawal. The Panama Canal Act of 1912, which prohibited railroad-owned ships from passing through the Canal in an endeavor to maintain transcontinental rail and water competition, destroyed Schwerin's plans for a combination of domestic traffic through the Canal and foreign trade with the Orient, because his line was owned by the Southern Pacific Company, operators of the Southern Pacific railway.

That the present absence of privately owned American cargo carriers in the trans-Pacific trade is due to the Seamen's Act is also questionable. With vessels of the Shipping Board available for charter on terms under which the government in effect underwrites any losses, it is hardly to be expected that private operators will seek to commence the operation of private ships on any considerable scale. The language test has not interfered seriously with the employment of Asiatic crews, which was the chief fear professed by Pacific shipowners. By permitting "pidgin English" orders and by using Chinese-English sailors' dictionaries to give the Orientals a smattering of English, the language test has been circumvented as a means of displacing the cheap Oriental crews. It seems very doubtful, then, that the present trans-Pacific shipping situation can be considered an effect of the Seamen's Act.

Is the Native American Returning to the Sea?

Whether the Seamen's Act is bringing the native American back to the sea cannot be definitely ascertained. It is certain, however, that, while the number of naturalized American seamen shipping before commissioners remained practically constant for the decade 1912–1920, the ratio of native born to naturalized advanced from less than 2 to 1 in 1910, and slightly over 2 to 1 in 1914, to over 4 to 1 in 1920, and over 3 to 1 in 1922. It must be recognized, however, that the war period was one of great expansion of our merchant marine, and that during that period foreign seamen in large numbers were not available. It is therefore impossible to determine what per cent of the increase of native-born seamen is due to the passage of the Seamen's Act.

Equalization of Foreign and American Wages

A question of great interest to both seamen and ship-owners is whether the Seamen's Act has operated to equalize foreign and American seamen's wages. The argument at the time of the passage of the act, it will be recalled, ran thus: Foreign seamen, under the sections mentioned, will no longer fear to leave their vessels in American ports for the purpose of reshipping at the higher rates prevailing here; by desertion, or the threat of desertion, they will force foreign masters to raise wages to the level prevailing in our ports; this action on their part will tend to equalize international competition in the matter of seamen's wages, help to keep an American merchant marine on the ocean, and build up a reserve of merchant seamen upon which the nation may draw in time of war. The seamen also hoped to benefit indirectly through more extensive employment, because of the disappearance of the wage differential against Americans and the opportunity to raise wages to yet higher levels. For the public, interest in the question arises from its bearing upon the granting of ship subsidies, the demand for which rests largely upon the ground of higher American wage costs.

The Half-Wages Clause

As late as December, 1919, the Pacific American Steamship Association asked the reimposition of imprisonment for desertion without cause in foreign countries. Further, they asked the repeal of the half-wages clause, both as regards American vessels and foreign vessels in American ports. These sections of the law are, of course, at the crux of the whole situation. Without them no equalization of wages could take place, a statement that finds expression in the following quotation from Raymond B. Stevens, vice-chairman of the Shipping Board during the war. Mr. Stevens also states that equalization has in fact resulted:

> I think the evidence clearly indicated that the La Follette Seamen's Act of 1915 has tended to increase wages paid by our foreign competitors; and the provision of this Act which makes that possible is the very provision that has been characterized as particularly vicious, the one that refers to a sailor's leaving the ship; and if that part of the law were stricken out, the law would not be as effective as it has been.

Positions of American Shipowners

In spite of this statement, American shipowners are loath to admit that the Seamen's Act has had any effect on foreign wages. For instance, A. F. Haines, vice-president of the Pacific Steamship Company, unequivocally denies the operation of such a tendency on the Pacific, and states that American owners import foreign crews to man ships out of American ports rather than pay American wages in the trans-Pacific trade. Judge Benjamin S. Grosscup, however, testifying as attorney for the same company, in response to questioning by Senator Fletcher, agreed with Mr. Stevens' statement that the tendency under the Seamen's Act is to raise wages to the American level. Furthermore, from the editorial columns of the *Pacific Marine Review* comes a clear statement that foreign seamen will leave their ships whenever possible to reship at higher rates.

> This decision will place foreign vessels at the Panama Canal on the same basis as American vessels so far as the part payment of wages earned is concerned, and will probably increase the number of desertions from foreign vessels, now comparatively few in number, with possibly a resulting increase in wages to the American scale on foreign vessels paying less.

This statement of John H. Rosseter on the point in question is unequivocal. His long experience as a private ship operator, and during the war period as director of operations of the Shipping Board, lends much authority to his opinion on shipping matters. In response to a question by Senator Simmons, of the Committee on Commerce, asking whether the La Follette Act had been one of the material factors in increasing foreign seamen's wages, he replied:

> I think it could be fairly stated that it has . . . with the exception of the Japanese. The Japanese, under the "gentlemen's agreement" have, up to this time, been restrained or influenced by their government from availing themselves of that act.

Foreign Shipowners

If some American shipowners scout the idea of wage equalization, foreign shipowners and even governments seem quite concerned about the effect of the half-wages clause. This was dramatically seen in the case of *Dillon v. Strathearn S. S. Co.* (252 U. S. 348), in which the British Embassy, the British shipowner, United States Attorney-General's office, and the British seaman asking half-wages (his case supported by the International Seamen's union of America), were all represented before the United States Supreme Court. In the case of *Thompson v. Lucas* (252 U. S. 358) the British shipowner's attorney made the following argument:

The only effect that the act has produced up to the present is that seamen on incoming vessels habitually demand one-half wages under it immediately upon arrival, and leave the ship at once. Crews are constantly changing, discipline is impaired, and unnecessary expenses are incurred.

The reader must not infer that American shipowners have dropped differences in wage costs from their arguments for government aid; that would be far from the fact. For instance, the *Pacific Marine Review* for February, 1922, prints a typical comparison of American and foreign wages showing a differential against American ships. This type of figures, however, should not be taken as having conclusive bearing on the operation of the Seamen's Act. In the first place, the American wages given are at the rate set May 1, 1921, a rate which was soon greatly undercut by private owners, especially on the Atlantic. In fact, ever since the expiration of the union agreements in 1921, the greatest variation in wage rates has prevailed. In the second place, foreign wages are not stated to be for vessels touching American ports. This point is fundamental, for it is only ships touching our ports that are affected by the Seamen's Act.

Foreign Seamen

Foreign seamen seem to be well informed of their rights under the American law, and are eager to take advantage of them. Foreign shipowners and masters, in an endeavor to hold their crews, have made threats of military service (during the war), discharged abroad men shipped in American ports at American wages, leaving the men stranded, have logged men who left ship as deserters and declared their wages forfeited, have refused to pay half-wages upon demand, and have made collection by the sailor as difficult as possible, and in many cases impossible.

All these obstructions have foreign interests placed in the way of wage equalization.

Shipping Board Investigation

In the summer of 1918, H. L. Gray, who made an investigation in England for the United States Shipping Board, wrote as follows:

The problem which, so far as crews are concerned, causes anxiety at the moment to the ministry of shipping is the retention of men in the British service. The higher wages offered to seamen in American vessels have led certain British crews who found themselves in American ports to go over to the more lucrative employment. To counteract this tendency the British ministry of shipping has since August, 1918, required that every member of a British crew provide himself with an "identity and Service" book, which he must be always ready to produce. Failure to show it or procure it exposes him to the operations of the military service acts. The important stipulation attached to this certificate is that the holder may not take service on the merchant vessels of any other nation. By this restrictive device it is hoped that the British crews may be retained intact despite the attraction of higher wages elsewhere.

This does not seem to have been wholly effective, for in October, 1918, a bonus of £3 a month was granted, but with the stipulation that it was not to be paid "to members of the crew signing on board on terms higher than the standard rates of pay." *Syren and Shipping,* a British nautical periodical, spoke of the increasing desertions of British seamen in American ports at that time, and noted that the fear of imprisonment and forfeiture of wages under British laws upon return to Britain is an insufficient deterrent. The reports of the Legal Aid Society of New York for 1916, 1917, 1918, and 1920 also record the fact of frequent desertion in New York in order to take advantage of the higher wages paid there, and the difficulties in getting half-wages for the deserting foreign seamen.

The fable of the contest between the wind and the sun

to remove the traveler's cloak, the one by blustering, the
other by smiling, evidently applies here, for it seems that
only by raising the wages of their seamen to the American
level are foreign ships able to hold their crews. In the
case of the British at least, this increase involved the
raising of seamen's wages largely in excess of the increases
paid in shore industries during the same period.

Shipping Board Conclusions

Two government investigations have been made to
ascertain whether the equalization of wages has been
taking place. The first, an investigation under the Industrial Relations Division of the Shipping Board of which
Robert P. Bass was director, reported as follows:

> The conclusion to be drawn from these figures would seem
> to be that, as far as the larger maritime nations are concerned,
> vessels touching at New York in December, 1918, were, with
> very few exceptions, in one way or another paying the American
> wage scale. The wages of American sailors had since 1914 gone
> up about 150 per cent and American firemen's wages about 90 per
> cent; but foreign wages had risen a much larger per cent and
> are now equal to the American rates.

Department of Labor Investigation

The other investigation was undertaken by the Investigation and Inspection Service of the Department of
Labor in the spring of 1919. Its report took special cognizance of the argument sometimes made that the rise in
foreign seamen's wages after 1915 was due solely to the
war, and not to the Seamen's Act.

> The investigation shows that a decided increase took place in
> seamen's wages everywhere after the enforcement of the Seamen's
> Act. Whether this increase was due in a larger measure to war
> conditions or to the change in the status of seamen in American
> ports in consequence of the Seamen's Act is impossible of cer-
> tain determination; but both factors contributed to this marked
> advance in wages. One circumstance, however, must be attributed
> to the Act alone. Seamen's wages have persistently followed the
> American standard. Unless restricted by governmental authority,

European wages at least have inclined toward equalization with the American wage rate, with the result that at the present time seamen's wages are not a deciding factor in competition among nations. It is only in respect of Japanese shipping that this result has not been attained.

Conclusion as to Wage Differentials

Summing up, there seems to be no alternative to the conclusion that the clause of the Seamen's Act designed to raise foreign seamen's wages to the American level has exhibited a tendency to operate as intended. This much has been ascertained by investigations, principally on the Atlantic coast. But because in the nature of things these conclusions must be somewhat tentative, the movements of wages during the next few years will still be of interest in this regard. The importance of wage differences in competition can easily be overemphasized by both subsidy proponents and those who stress the economic significance of wage equalization under the Seamen's Act. Assuming that wage costs are 15 per cent of *operating* costs, not total costs (Edward N. Hurley, chairman of the United States Shipping Board during the war, estimated them to be 12 per cent), and that the American wages bill is 25 per cent higher than that of the foreign competitor, the disadvantage to the American operator would be less than 4 per cent of operating costs. Officers' wages form a considerable proportion of the wages bill and are not directly affected by the Seamen's Act. The seamen claim that when foreign seamen's wages rise toward the American level, their officers' wages will likewise rise to maintain present differentials. No evidence specifically supporting this contention has yet been adduced

Alien Seamen in American Ports

The objection of the longshoremen who opposed the seamen's bill was based upon the fear that the same provisions which were intended to equalize wages would flood the waterfronts of our ports with unemployed foreign seamen. Some thousands of alien seamen were left stranded on Atlantic and Gulf ports during 1921, but this condition was due to the wholesale laying up of ships on account of the prevailing depression; the Seamen's Act had nothing to do with it. A report of the New York Legal Aid Society in 1917, also, seems to indicate that instances of that kind took place for a time at least. The Legal Aid Society of New York reported in 1917:

A large number of seamen of every nationality have been thrown upon the labor market at American ports, and this condition necessarily helps to keep down the wage scale at American ports.

Whether such a condition proved or will prove to be general seems doubtful. Some foreign ships may go out short-handed, but on the whole it would seem that ships losing crews must replace them, thus restoring the original balance between demand and supply. Furthermore, in many, perhaps most, cases, the threat of desertion will prove sufficient to compel the raise in wages. That ships do clear short-handed, however, especially in case of strikes, was clearly demonstrated on the Great Lakes during the strike of 1922, when vessels unable to get full crews cleared port without them, and were permitted to do so by Department of Commerce inspector under a ruling approved by the Attorney-General. The seamen are now endeavoring to prevent a ship from sailing without a full crew and to compel foreign vessels to fill deserters' places at American wages. To this end a bill has been introduced in Congress providing that no ship shall depart on a voyage to a foreign port with fewer in her crew than she had when she arrived. It is argued that this provision will also assist in checking violations of the immigration laws which have been especially prevalent since the 3 per cent limit went into effect. The violations are frequently made by persons who ship ostensibly as seamen and then desert, but who in reality are immigrants and not seamen at all. This problem of the relation between the section of the Seamen's Act which permits alien seamen to demand half-wages and come ashore and the enforcement of the immigration laws has caused some administrative problems, but the Commissioner General of Immigration has repeatedly stated that "the provisions of the immigration law and regulations affecting seamen could be enforced in such a manner as not to interfere with the operations of the Seamen's Act."

Wage Equalization on the Pacific

As indicated above, equalization has taken place principally at Atlantic ports. On the Pacific coast foreign seamen have not fully availed themselves of the provisions of the Seamen's Act. The preference of American shipowners for Oriental crews at a lower wage rate rather than American crews at American wages; differences in American and Oriental standards of living; the Chinese exclusion laws, and the rule requiring $500 bond of Chinese seamen going ashore, the validity of which is being tested in the courts; the restraint of Japanese seamen for fear of giving offense on the ground of violating the "gentlemen's agreement"; the influence brought to bear upon Japanese seamen by American seamen's leaders in urging them to postpone taking advantage of the law pending decisions of the United States Supreme Court upon the validity of the half-wage clause as it affects foreign vessels; all these factors have prevented the full operation of the act, and the realization of its benefits in the equalization of wages in trans-Pacific shipping. It is claimed that the Japanese shipowners will prove especially vulnerable because of the language clause, the absence of Japanese seamen in the United States, and the greater incentive of the poorly paid Japanese sailor to desert. On the other hand, the language clause will prevent Japanese from reshipping on any except Japanese vessels. Whether these obstacles will do more than postpone the equalization of wages on the Pacific, it is too early to predict.

Efforts to Amend Seamen's Act

Almost every session of Congress sees attempts to amend the Seamen's Act in one way or another. The Rowe bill, sought to reduce the experience qualifications of an able seaman to six weeks' training aboard a Shipping Board training vessel and six months' training on a merchant vessel, or six months aboard a merchant vessel followed by the examination given on board the Shipping Board training vessel. This amendment, however, failed to become law. The Merchant Marine Act of 1920 made three amendments to the Seamen's Act. The Seamen's Act had permitted men to demand half-wages every five days even when the ship lay in a port of loading or discharging cargo longer than five days. The amendment provided that the men should not be entitled to half-wages more than once in the same harbor on the same entry. Allotments made in foreign ports were prohibited by this same act, as a final blow to the crimps, and the Federal Employers' Liability Act modifying the employers' defenses in case of personal injury to employees was extended to seamen. Senator Johnson, of California, introduced a workmen's compensation bill for seamen, but it was later withdrawn at the instance of the seamen themselves, because it took away the right of injured seamen to sue for damages. This right was felt to be important in cases of serious injury where the amount of compensation fixed by law was inadequate. The sailors want a compensation law, but with the right of electing the remedy after the injury.

In the last Congress (67th) the seamen introduced several measures intended to strengthen the Seamen's Act, but were not successful in securing their passage. Perhaps the most important of these proposals is the one denying to shipowners their present limitation of liability in case the vessel violated any of the laws for safety at sea or sailed inefficiently or insufficiently manned. This provision is intended to enlist the financial interest of the shipowners on the side of strict enforcement of the clauses of the Seamen's Act dealing with safety and manning, instead of relying, as at present, on government inspection. The seamen also propose that no signing on or paying off of seamen shall be done unless the vessel is connected with the shore by a gangway. The reason urged is one recognized in a recent decision by Judge Hanford, namely, that the element of coercion cannot be excluded when articles are signed aboard a vessel lying in the stream. The *Pacific Marine Review* points out that: "Thus would be prevented the hiring of crews in cases of strikes and delivery of the men to a ship in the stream." Both contentions are probably true.

And so the contest goes on. The "old man of the sea" still remains in Washington fighting every amendment which may vitiate the La Follette Act and proposing measures of his own that will ensure its enforcement.

CHAPTER IX

THE WAR AND AFTER[1]

Early Effects of War on the Pacific

The effects of the European War were slow to be felt by the sailors on the Pacific. For nearly two years after the outbreak of the war, wages of seamen on the Pacific coast remained the same as prior to 1914. Then, on May 1, 1916, union wages rose by agreement to $55 a month on steam vessels. Wages in sailing vessels on the coast and to Mexico and the Hawaiian Islands were set at $50, and for offshore voyages, $40. With the entry of the United States into the war, however, the building and manning of an immense merchant marine became a problem of the first magnitude and of pressing urgency. The cry was for "ships, ships, and then ships," and its corollary was "seamen, seamen, and then seamen," for the pre-war personnel was wholly inadequate in numbers, and foreign sailors were in great demand on vessels of their own countries. In the emergency the government sought and received the co-operation of shipowners and seamen.

Sailors, Shipowners, and the War

Andrew Furuseth did not believe in our entry into the war. Nevertheless, he took the position that it was the duty of seamen to aid to the best of their ability the

---

[1] Sources for this chapter include pamphlets issued by shipowners, sailors, and marine transport workers, and personal interviews. Also:
  Report of United States Shipping Board (see page 110).
  Proceedings of International Seamen's Union.
  Seamen's Journal and the *Pacific Marine Review.*

nation which had given them freedom (not forgetting, however, to keep an eye on the shipowners). How well the sailors served the country is indicated by the fact that the seamen were one of the few classes of labor that worked continuously throughout the war without any strikes.

The only threatened interruption was on the Great Lakes where the seamen threatened to strike in order to force the Lake Carriers' Association, dominated by a subsidiary of the United States Steel Corporation, to enter into an agreement with the unions and the government similar to the so-called Atlantic agreement described below, and to compel the abolition of the grade book system. This trouble was averted when a number of the owners outside the association agreed to co-operate, and the United States Shipping Board, after investigation, ordered the abolition of the continuous discharge books. The Lake Carriers' Association accepted the decision of the Shipping Board on the grade books and wages, and signed the joint appeal for seamen agreed to by the Atlantic shipowners, but refused to enter into an agreement which might be construed as recognition of the unions.

Atlantic Agreement

The war policies of the nation affecting seamen were determined by agreement underwritten by the government, between the shipowners sitting on the Shipping Committee of the Council of National Defense and the International Seamen's Union of America. The first of these was the so-called Atlantic agreement, tentatively approved May 8 and ratified on August 8, 1917. This tripartite war agreement was the first of its kind in the

United States. The main object of the agreement was to provide for the expansion of the American merchant marine to meet war needs, especially to ensure the necessary increase and efficiency of its personnel. Under this agreement the Shipping Board and the shipowners agreed to pay a standard scale of wages, war bonuses, and compensation for losses of personal effects, and agreed to the joint issuance of an appeal for merchant seamen. The representatives of the seamen's unions were granted free access to the docks and vessels.

The seamen, on their part, voluntarily agreed to a dilution of labor, allowing 40 per cent of the deck crews to be made up of ordinary seamen or boys, that is, apprentices and graduates of the Shipping Board training ships who were drawn in to man the new merchant marine. The seamen further agreed to use earnest efforts in co-operation with the officers to teach seamanship to the ordinary seamen and apprentices. The seamen thus voluntarily accepted a condition less favorable to union labor than existed before the war, especially on the Pacific coast, where the sailors were about 95 per cent organized. On the other hand, they gained formal recognition by the owners on the Atlantic.

Pacific Agreement

The Atlantic agreement, which has just been set forth in detail, applied only to the Atlantic and Gulf districts, but the method employed on the Pacific for the dilution of labor was similar to that embodied in the Atlantic agreement. On the Pacific coast, shipowners and unions made agreements concerning wages and working rules in much the same fashion as before the war, and the Shipping Board accepted those wage rates for its vessels operating on the Pacific.

Training New Sailors

Under these plans the Shipping Board began the training of crews in January, 1918. Inexperienced men were enrolled at 6,854 official enrolling stations at drug stores throughout the country, were sent to the training stations for an average of six weeks' intensive training, and then sent to sea in the proportion of four ordinary seamen to six able seamen. In this way the Sea Service Bureau of the Shipping Board trained and placed on board American ships 9,523 seamen, 9,053 firemen, and 5,333 employees of the steward's department.

The International Seamen's Union of America, in addition to the appeal for seamen sent out jointly with the shipowners and government, issued a ringing "Call to the Sea," in the name of the country's need and the freedom which American sailors had been the first to receive.

To All Seafaring Men Ashore or Afloat

The nation that proclaimed your freedom now needs your services. America is at war. Our troops are being transported over the sea. Munitions and supplies are being shipped in ever increasing quantities to our armies in Europe. The bases are the ports of America. The Battlefields are in Europe. The sea intervenes. Over it the men of the sea must sail the supply ships. A great emergency fleet is now being built. . . . Your help is needed to prove that no enemy on the seas can stop the ships of the nation whose seamen bear the responsibility of liberty.

America has the right, a far greater right than any other nation, to call upon the seamen of all the world for service. By responding to this call now you can demonstrate your practical appreciation of freedom won.

Stirring War Hatred of Seamen by Seamen Opposed

At the same time that Furuseth was thus patriotically urging support of the war by American seamen, and coöperating loyally with the government, he never forgot his devotion to all seamen regardless of nationality. This spirit of devotion is finely shown in his reply to an invita-

tion to a seamen's conference in Great Britain, called for
the purpose of condemning the German seamen's support
of the submarine policy.

. . . . no action taken by the seamen, as such, could influence the
policy. Our chief concern ought to be directed to prevent any
hatred of seamen by seamen. Seamen have no choice but to
obey. He is not morally responsible for his action under command
in war. By hating he will become morally responsible. Hatred
once developed does not cease with the war and it will then be
used by shipowners to pit seamen against seamen in the economic
struggle.

Wages and Conditions in War Time and Later

Stimulated by the war, unparalleled shipping activity
sent wages of seamen upward. On May 1, 1917, wages
on all vessels and in all trades rose by agreement to $60,
and on March 1 of the following year the scale was set
at $75. In August, 1919, the return of tonnage to the
Pacific after the slackening of war needs in the Atlantic,
and the corresponding scarcity of sailors, sent the agreed
scale of wages on the Pacific coast up to $90 a month.
The 8-hour day in port, and at sea in steamers, was
secured, and overtime was paid for at the rate of 75 cents
an hour for ship work, and 90 cents an hour for working
cargo. Individual members not infrequently demanded
and received more than this scale when post-war prosperity was at its height and men were scarce. Yet, notwithstanding the rapidity of the rise of wages of seamen,
wages did not begin to keep pace with the phenomenal
flight of war freight rates.

With the spring of 1921 came business depression,
and consequent slackening of shipping activity. Inasmuch as the agreements between shipowners and seamen
expired on May 1 of that year, shipowners on all coasts
and the Shipping Board took steps looking toward a
reduction of wages on the grounds of the decline of

marine shipping, the competition of foreign vessels, and the decline in living costs. The demands placed before the seamen included a reduction of able seamen's wages to $72.50 a month and the abolition of all overtime, as "foreign to the spirit and customs of the sea." The American Steamship Owners' Association, the Pacific American Association, and the Shipowners' Association of the Pacific Coast agreed to the wages and conditions laid down by Admiral Benson, chairman of the Shipping Board. This decision, of course, was a severe blow to the monthly earnings of seamen, inasmuch as it both reduced pay, and stopped overtime, which was an important source of income, especially on the lumber vessels of the Pacific coast, where much of the cargo work is done on overtime. The Shipping Board's only substitute for overtime was that "for work performed in excess of 8 hours, equivalent time off will be given."

Marine Strike of 1921

The International Seamen's Union, together with the Marine Engineers' Beneficial Association, refused to accept these cuts in wages and conditions. At the last moment they asked for arbitration, but the Shipping Board and the owners refused. On May 1, the strike began.

The conduct of the strike was marked by violence along the waterfronts, and some cases of sabotage, such as emery dust put into the engine bearings of vessels which put to sea in spite of the strike. On the Pacific coast the use of students of the University of California as strike breakers occasioned much bitterness. The Shipping Board was active in securing injunctions against the unions, and sent more ships to sea with non-union crews than did the owners. The sailors felt greatly aggrieved that the government was using the ships "bought and paid for by the Liberty bonds of the people" to fight the battle of private owners and to carry strike breakers.

Slack shipping conditions, the hostility of the government, and the existence of a large surplus of war-trained sailors willing to fill the places of the striking seamen foredoomed the seamen's efforts to failure. Before the strike had been long in progress, President Brown of the Marine Engineers decided to sign the agreement. His own organization protested vehemently, especially the engineers on the Pacific coast, but on account of his action they practically had to go back, leaving the fight to the seamen.

The Steam Schooner Offer

On the Pacific coast the Shipowners' Association, controlling most of the vessels in the coasting lumber trade, made little or no attempt to operate, leaving the Shipping Board and the larger owners to conduct the strike, which was now on a frankly open-shop basis. In July, however, the Shipowners' Association broke away from the American Steamship Owners, and Pacific American Steamship Association, and offered the sailors $77.50 a month, 60 cents an hour overtime, and the maintenance of union working conditions, with an informal open-shop agreement for one year. The steam schooners of the association employ probably over half of the seamen on the coast; consequently their crews have been the backbone of the Sailors' Union, and the unionization of the steam schooners has always been of prime importance to the union. Coming at a time when the engineers had deserted, and when the strike was practically lost, it seemed that this offer was just so much salvage from the wreck. Furuseth, at that time in Washington, wired the union advising acceptance. Most of the other officers of the union were likewise in favor of the offer.

But one of the clauses in the proposed agreement stipulated that sailors should work with longshoremen, regardless of the latter's affiliation or non-affiliation with a union. Now such a clause, although not perhaps palatable to seamen as part of an agreement, was nevertheless not far out of harmony with the traditional union policy toward longshoremen as both practiced and preached. Yet this agreement, which would have aided the union and its members so materially, and would have saved them from further reductions for a year, was voted down against the advice of all but two of the officers, by the overwhelming majority of 1,607 to 118. The internal situation responsible for this will be set forth presently.

Termination of Strike

Affairs having taken this turn, Furuseth hastened back from Washington, and immediately upon his arrival addressed the membership of his union at a special meeting assembled in the San Francisco Civic Auditorium. In his powerful and effective fashion he set before the men the facts of the worldwide depression and tying up of ships, showing them the futility of further resistance, whether in alliance with longshoremen or anybody else. So convincingly and forcibly did the old Norseman present the case, that the same membership which only three weeks before had voted down the shipowners' offer now by a count of two to one voted to end the strike and return to work with no agreement whatever.

Further Wage Reduction

With the continuance of the depression, further reductions of wages were put into effect, although they did not fall so low as on the Atlantic. The Shipowners' Association reduced wages of able seamen in the lumber schooners from $72.50 to $65 in February, 1922. Wages in sailing vessels were at the same time set at $50 in Pacific coast voyages and to the Hawaiian Islands and $40 in all other voyages. The Pacific American Steamship Association cut wages on February 1 to $55. But of greater lasting importance to sailors was the establishment by the owners' associations of a shipping office commonly known among seamen as the "slave market," and the reintroduction of the grade book system. The control of shipping men once more passed from the hands of the union to the owners.

It was not many months before coastwise shipping activity returned, especially in the lumber trade. As a result, wages began to move upward during the latter part of 1922 and the first half of 1923. But the owners' control of shipping remained.

Internal Conflict

Within the union, too, significant movements were taking place. While Furuseth was in Washington during the strike, a group hostile to his policies began to agitate its views and to gain adherents. The success which attended their efforts may be judged by the overwhelming rejection of the shipowners' offer mentioned above. This revolt, for it developed into a real revolt, was composed of twa elements.

First there were those who carried I. W. W. cards, who at first secretly and later openly sought to capture the union for the I. W. W. The potential value of the seamen to the I. W. W. is great, both as a means of spreading propaganda to all corners of the world, and because of the economic power wielded by any group strong enough to bring transportation to a standstill. The other group was composed of non-I. W. W. who favored the formation of a marine transportation workers' federation as a means of increasing their economic power.

The mouthpiece of this revolt was Vance Thompson, editor of the *Seamen's Journal,* not an I. W. W. but a member of the Sailors' Union of long standing, who years before had edited the *Journal* for a few months. In 1920, by a narrow margin, he defeated Scharrenberg, against whom he had personal enmity. The International Seamen's Union at its next convention, anticipating a change in editorial policy, withdrew from the *Journal* the right to speak as its official organ. This added bitterness to the feeling between the Furuseth-Scharrenberg group and the discontented members now led by Thompson. By the time the strike was well under way the *Journal* was printing editorials advocating industrial unionism, setting forth the evils of the traditional union policies, and bearing such headlines as "Marine Transport Workers Awake."

Under Thompson's leadership the union passed a resolution favoring close affiliation with the longshoremen, and a committee was sent to confer with the Riggers' and Stevedores' Union. When the steam schooner owners made their offer of a separate peace, Thompson centered all the power of his pen and oratory on the section of the offer which required sailors to work with union and non-union longshoremen alike. With the union spirit of the sailors already at a high pitch because of the strike, and with the demand for a closer affiliation with marine workers already stimulated, it was easy to play up this section as an agreement to "scab" on the longshoremen. As a matter of fact, it represented the policy which sailors and longshoremen have usually followed. Thompson swept all opposition before him, however, and secured the almost unanimous rejection of the offer. This astounding defeat brought Furuseth back from Washington to make the speech which turned the tide in the opposite direction and persuaded the sailors to go back to work by a vote of two to one.

The Revolt Crushed

The Marine Transport Workers' Union No. 510 (I. W. W.) was now working openly to win over the seamen. Furuseth accepted the gage of battle which they threw down, and determined to rid his union of I. W. W.'s. Feeling between Thompson and Furuseth grew more intense. The International Seamen's Union began publishing a paper, *The Seaman,* of which four issues appeared, defying the I. W. W. and attacking the "irresponsible editor" of the *Seamen's Journal.* This provoked Thompson to more violent attacks in reply, notwithstanding a resolution warning against them passed by the union at Furuseth's insistence. The battle ended with the preferment of charges and counter-charges, and the final expulsion of Thompson by a two-thirds vote. He was succeeded by Selim A. Silver, a prominent Furuseth adherent who had served as business manager under Scharrenberg and Thompson. The expulsion of Thompson on grounds of disobedience was followed by the expulsion of a considerable number of the insurgents accused of membership in the I. W. W., in vigorous enforcement of the provision in the union constitution prohibiting membership in any dual organization. The internal revolt was crushed and Furuseth was again in complete control of the policies of his own union. To avoid repetition of some of the experiences during the struggle, the union constitution was carefully overhauled. The chairman was made a permanent officer of the union, instead of being elected at each meeting; the process of expulsion for membership in a dual union was made easier; and by vote of the Sailors' Union, the *Seamen's Journal* was turned over to the International Seamen's Union.

Marine Transport Workers

The conflict within the Sailors' Union had ended. Nevertheless it continued on the waterfronts and vessels of all our coasts. The Marine Transport Workers maintained offices in principal ports, and waged a battle of pamphlets against the "obsolete" craft unionism of Furuseth, who vigorously carried on the attack in a series of pamphlets of his own. He brought to bear every available argument. He compared the constitution of the Marine Transport Workers and the International Seamen's Union section by section. He warned of the danger of prosecution under the California criminal syndicalism law, a danger threatening not only individuals, but the Sailors' Union itself should it, under I. W. W. domination, become a proscribed organization and the seamen be diverted from their program because of prosecution by the state or through being led astray by the dream of an "impossible" changing of human society.

We seamen have other work to do. . . . It is our duty, as it was our promise in our hours of bondage, to assist other seamen to become at least as free as we are. This can only be accomplished by working to this end within the law.

He added to his other arguments his belief that the I. W. W. was in the pay of the employers and that its tactics were dictated by detective organizations, supporting his belief by the testimony brought out by Frank P. Walsh, and the testimony given by Basil Manly. So bitter, indeed, became Furuseth's hostility that he resigned from the American Civil Liberties Union, an organization which sought to maintain the rights of free speech, free press,

and free assemblage and which spent much of its efforts
in defending I. W. W.'s (as well as the Ku Klux Klan).
While asserting his belief in these civil liberties, he nevertheless said, "I cannot fight for human rights in company
with the I. W. W."

On April 25, 1923, the I. W. W. called a general strike
of marine workers, lumberjacks, and oil workers on the
Pacific coast. The Sailors' Union, of course, refused to
participate for its members were already "working the
oracle" with some success. The tie-up proved fairly effective in the lumber camps of the northwest and among the
longshoremen in San Pedro. Some vessels were delayed,
particularly in the offshore trade.

Returning Strength of the Sailors' Union

Neither union has published statistics of membership
recently, but it seems probable that the Sailors' Union
will continue to regain strength, especially in the lumber
schooners, which have always been its stronghold. The
conflict is not over, however. The International Seamen's
Union realizes this and continues its attack, bent on crushing the opposition which reared its head as the seamen
were going down to defeat before shipowners and the
Shipping Board.

British Columbia Seamen

Organizations of seamen in British Columbia and
extensions of the Sailors' Union of the Pacific into that
field deserve some separate consideration in addition to
the general union history which has been traced in these
pages.

On October 19, 1891, the first British Columbia branch
of the Sailors' Union was founded in Victoria. The purpose of this move was to unionize the men in the British

Columbia–California coal trade which was then flourishing, and to serve as an outpost to keep non-union sailors away from the United States. The agency was of assistance in organizing the men sailing from British Columbia ports, particularly the sealers of Victoria in 1892. Later the agency moved to Nanaimo, and in 1895 was closed, the chief reason being the extremities to which the Sailors' Union was at that time reduced.

British Columbia Seamen's Own Unions

British Columbia seamen have tried unions of their own. The Mainland Steamshipmen's Union at one time affiliated with the International Seamen's Union of America, but dropped out because of non-payment of dues. In 1902 the Sailors' Union arranged for interchange of membership cards with the British Columbia Steamshipmen's Society, but this proved of little value to either organization. The British Columbia union was disrupted the following year in a sympathetic strike with the United Brotherhood of Railway Employees.

Re-establishment of Sailors' Union Branches in British Columbia

During the strike of 1906 it was found that the shipowners got most of their skilled non-union men from British Columbia. As a result, there was agitation for a British Columbia branch, which ended in the establishment of an agency at Vancouver in April, 1908. British Columbia men were admitted to the branch of the Sailors' Union for a $1 fee, but their cards were not recognized in American vessels except upon payment of the full initiation fee of $5. The reasons which prompted this move into British Columbia were, first, to protect the membership in the United States against the influx of unorganized, skilled seamen; second, to protect the wages of the men who sail from the American side to Alaska against competition because of lower wage and operating costs on goods sent from the United States via the Canadian Pacific Railway under bond to a British Columbia port, and thence on British Columbia vessels; a third reason was the duty which trade unionists generally feel of organizing the unorganized of their craft and aiding in improving their conditions. In 1913 it was further decided to organize the marine firemen, oilers, and watertenders in British Columbia as a part of the International Seamen's Union.

National prejudice hampered the work of organizing the Sailors' Union branch in Vancouver, and it has remained a factor in the situation, the British Columbia branches exhibiting an independence of headquarters in San Francisco not found in the United States branches. When the Vancouver agency was founded in 1908, wages were $30 and $35. By 1911 they were raised to $45 and $50 with partial recognition of overtime after ten hours. In July, 1917, between 500 and 600 sailors and firemen went out on strike demanding the same wages as on the United States side, which were then $60. In two weeks they had won a partial victory in the form of a 15 per cent increase. In June, 1919, the Vancouver branch decided to take a strike vote, to which headquarters objected. The matter was settled, however, when the owners agreed to the demands of $75 a month, the 8-hour day in port, and three watches, accomplishing the same result, at sea. A week later the branches, against the wishes of headquarters, joined a sympathetic general strike in Vancouver which was the outgrowth of the Winnipeg general strike. The result of such action was, of course, to irritate and cause friction among all parties concerned—the owners, headquarters of the Sailors' Union, and the British Columbia branches themselves. At that time there was considerable sentiment in the British Columbia branches toward withdrawal from the Sailors' Union, some members being in favor of seeking an independent charter from the International Seamen's Union, others being in favor of affiliation with the One Big Union. When the matter came to a vote, separation was decisively defeated. Nevertheless, the Sailors' Union has had difficulty in maintaining its always precarious hold on British Columbia seamen. In July, 1920, the Victoria branch was closed, and a "wobbly" rival is in the field, the Canadian Sailors', Firemen's, and Cooks' Union.

Relations of Sailors' Union and British Columbia Branch

The history of the British Columbia branches shows that they have a distinctive relation to the Sailors' Union in fact if not in form. National prejudices, different laws governing seamen, differences in ports and territory served, and differences in temper of the labor movement ashore have contributed to this situation. On the whole, however, the points of common interest seem of much greater importance than the points of difference, although it is by no means certain that Canadian seamen will see the matter in this light. The friction and lack of harmony manifested is of minor importance when viewed beside the advantages which have come to the British Columbia seamen in the form of better wages, hours, conditions, and stability of organization since the establishment of the Sailors' Union of the Pacific branch in British Columbia.

CHAPTER X

ORGANIZATION AND POLICIES[1]

Centralized Craft Unionism

The Coast Seamen's Union developed a unique type of organization, which is continued in the Sailors' Union of today. Like most unions of shore workers, it is based on craft lines, only members of the deck department of vessels being eligible. But unlike shore unions, the Sailors' Union is not made up of independent locals. There is but one Sailors' Union for the entire Pacific coast, a centralized craft union with headquarters at San Francisco and branches at those ports along the coast where crews are most commonly shipped.

Headquarters and Branches

The difference between headquarters and the branches is principally in the degree of authority possessed. Headquarters is the seat of the main offices of the union and the place where the records are kept. Committees from headquarters ordinarily conduct the negotiations for agreements with shipowners. Branches are conducted by agents, who are elected by vote of the entire union membership just as the other union officers are elected. Agents and branches are under the immediate jurisdiction of headquarters meetings. They are chiefly useful as a means of controlling the shipping of men in ports up and down the coast, and of providing a rendezvous for union seamen where they can meet, discuss union problems, and vote

---

[1] Material in this chapter taken from constitution and minutes of the Sailors' Union, the *Seamen's Journal,* and from personal interviews with seamen and longshoremen.

upon matters submitted to the entire membership. They also aid in keeping up the membership of the union by collecting dues and by inducing non-unionists to join. Branches have no power to call strikes, although members may vote on strikes in the branches.

Most important of all in the centralization of authority in the headquarters at San Francisco is the fact that headquarters meeting possesses an absolute veto on the acts of the branches. No action taken, nor rule adopted by a branch, is valid until endorsed by a meeting at headquarters.

The reason for this peculiar organization lies in the fact that the seaman is the most migratory of all workers. His calling takes him everywhere. In whatever port his voyage ends he must seek employment on another vessel. Obviously, any organization claiming jurisdiction over him must be co-extensive with his field of employment. Among industrial workers ashore this condition of successful organization is satisfied by the local union. Among the migratory agricultural laborers and lumberjacks the universal card of the I. W. W. makes headway where the local fails. Among sailors the centralized craft union has developed, with unrestricted exchange of membership between recognized seamen's unions of other coasts and nations.

Craft Industrialism

In many ways, however, the sailors conduct their activities upon an industrial, rather than a craft basis. This is secured through affiliation with the International Seamen's Union of America, which is, in effect, an industrial union, or more accurately, it is an example of craft industrialism, i.e., a federation of all the craft unions in the industry. The Sailors' Union voluntarily co-operates with the Marine Firemen's, and Marine Cooks' and Stewards' Unions of the Pacific. This co-operation is informal and verbal, but close, because based upon community of interests, and because of the fact that they are all members of the International Seamen's Union. The three unions, whose members work together on the same vessels, collaborate in their demands on the owners. They negotiate together and strike together, although the final agreements between the owners and each union are separate. Likewise their representatives have fought together for the same legislation improving the status of seamen.

Co-operation Among Unions of Seamen

The Sailors' Union also co-operates with the Atlantic and Lake Unions, especially the former. These unions, too, are affiliated with the International Seamen's Union. The co-operation in this case is not in making agreements with the owners, but in helping to unionize the crews of vessels coming from or going to the other coast. This mutual service is especially valuable in time of strikes. In 1921, when the Shipping Board and shipowners from all coasts stood together for a wage reduction, the seamen of all coasts likewise united in striking to oppose it. The legislative program outlined by Andrew Furuseth, of the Sailors' Union of the Pacific, has always been carried on in the name of the International Seamen's Union, and with minor exceptions, has been loyally supported by the organized seamen from all parts of the country.

Union Committees

The Sailors' Union has always prided itself upon the democracy of its organization. There is no standing executive committee which passes on matters of policy and brings its recommendation to the meeting to be ratified. Matters must be threshed out in open meeting, or referred to a committee elected by the meeting to consider the particular proposal. The only regular committees are the banking, finance, and auditing committees, and an emergency committee composed of the officers, who act only when an urgent difficulty arises demanding attention before a meeting can be called, and whose actions are subject to review or change by the headquarters meeting. This democracy gives all shades of opinion, including rebellious elements, the opportunity of airing their views and often hinders the expeditious transaction of business, but this is considered preferable to greater concentration of authority in the hands of a small group of officers. Until 1922 a chairman was elected at each meeting of the union. This action was taken partly in the interests of democracy in the conduct of meetings, partly for the purpose of training as many members as possible in parliamentary procedure. As a matter of practice, however, the selection of presiding officer was generally made from the same group of fifteen or twenty men who were most familiar with parliamentary rules, for it was difficult to induce inexperienced members to accept the position. Following the recent insurgent movement within the union, however, when contests over the position of chairman for the evening were many and bitter, and when one of those elected was later found not to be in good standing, the chairman has again been made a permanent official, elected for the same term as the other officers of the union.

Officers

The secretary is the executive officer of the union. In their respective localities the branch agents exercise a similar office. The patrolmen, assigned to regular districts about the harbor, perform functions similar to those of walking delegates ashore, ascertaining whether the crews of vessels in the harbor are members of the union in good standing, and endeavoring to build up the membership of the union and to prevent the shipping of non-union seamen. They also visit each week any members who may be sick in the hospital. When the union had agreements with the owners, the patrolmen appointed from among the crew of each out-bound vessel a member to act as ship's delegate. The duty of the ship's delegate was, when overtime was worked, to compare time with the officer in charge after knocking off. He also acted as representative of the men in presenting grievances to the officers.

Benefits

The Sailors' Union of the Pacific is primarily a labor organization of the business union type, not a benevolent association. In Furuseth's words, the sailors "are not running a Red Cross Society." Nevertheless it performs no inconsiderable services for its members which it classes as "benefits." Reading rooms are maintained where members may gather to read or to discuss matters of common interest. Each member in good standing formerly received a weekly copy of the *Seamen's Journal*. Since the internal troubles of 1921 over the question of industrial unionism, the *Seamen's Journal* has been transferred to the International Seamen's Union, which now issues it as a monthly publication. While the distribution of the *Journal* is classed as a "benefit," and is one in a sense, still the *Journal* is first and foremost the publicity weapon of the union. Without doubt one of the best papers published by organized labor anywhere, the value of its services can hardly be overestimated in maintaining the morale of the union in times of stress, in welding the members of the craft together for common purposes, in providing a channel for the dissemination of information and news affecting the seamen and organized labor in general, in expanding the organization of seamen, and in providing publicity for the cause of the seamen.

A shipwreck benefit to aid members who have lost clothing in shipwrecks, fire, or similar accidents during the course of their employment is maintained for all members in good standing. Its purpose is not to provide complete insurance against loss, but merely to enable the shipwrecked sailor to buy sufficient clothes to go to sea again. This feature is as old as the Coast Seamen's Union, when the shipwreck fund was maintained on the basis of a voluntary contribution of 25 cents, and later $1 a year. At the present time, the shipwreck benefit, like all the other benefits, is included in the $1 a month dues. The maximum that can be paid under the benefit is now $75.

Deceased members, if in good standing at the time of death, and if death occurs at or near headquarters or any branch, are buried by the union, the expense not to exceed $85. Members sick in hospitals are entitled to $1 a week for hospital supplies. Members who have been admitted to Sailors' Snug Harbor to spend their declining years are entitled to transportation to New York. During strikes, members out of employment for more than two weeks as a result of the strike, who report to the union daily and perform such duties as may be required of them, are entitled to a strike benefit of not more than $5 weekly.

Donations

The Sailors' Union has frequently extended financial aid to other bodies of organized labor in trouble, although it has never asked money for itself. Its minutes are filled with records of donations to unions of all kinds, ranging from bakers to steel workers, from longshoremen to their fellow seamen in the International Seamen's Union. The largest single donation was $25,000 to the Great Lakes Seamen's Union. For the 17-year period 1891–1908, donations averaged slightly over $1,000 a year.

Membership in the Sailors' Union is limited to practical sailors who are either American citizens or are eligible to citizenship. Candidates are required to pass an examination in seamanship to determine their rating. If they do not qualify as able seamen, they may be admitted as ordinary seamen. But the policy of the union is to advise such men to sail as ordinary seamen until they can qualify as able seamen and join the union as such. The initiation fee is kept at the low figure of $5, and dues $1 a month, in order that no one may be kept out for financial reasons. In 1920 the seamen on the Pacific coast were practically 100 per cent organized, with a membership of 6,500. The present membership figures have not been made public.

Methods of Recruiting Membership

The union follows various methods in securing members. As already stated, it is one of the regular duties of patrolmen to ascertain whether the crews of all vessels are members of the union. If not they attempt to induce them to become so. When "scabbing" becomes frequent, and the patrolman cannot prevent it (or when struggling with the shipowners), the device known as "dummies" or "the oracle," described in Chapters IV and VIII, is sometimes resorted to to bring pressure on the owners shipping non-union crews. It can be used by individual seamen or groups of seamen to considerable effect without involving a union strike declaration against all vessels. As used by dissatisfied, even though unorganized, sailors, it may be made the source of considerable annoyance to shipowners. Essentially, the tactics are the same as the sudden strike, or the strike in detail in any shore occupation. Although the owners have tried to brand it as sabotage, it is wholly unlike that practice, and is doubtless perfectly legal.

The closed shop is enforced whenever possible. At such times as it is in force men desiring to sail come to the union office voluntarily and apply for membership. When union men find themselves aboard ship with non-union men, they persuade the latter to join. If that fails (when the union is strong), they threaten to leave. This usually has the desired effect, for the captain does not wish to lose his crew, and unless the non-union man does join he is likely to find himself out of a job. Files of the San Francisco newspapers and tales of the past indicate that somewhat more vigorous methods have at times been used to bring in men who subsequently became most loyal members. If it is not possible to maintain the closed shop, union men are commonly allowed to sail with non-union men with a view to persuading the latter to join the union and also to keep down the number of non-union men sailing. Organizers are sometimes sent out by the union to build up the membership. There are none on the Pacific at the present time, but when they are sent out, they serve in much the same way as the patrolmen, using the particular methods that seem best adapted to the situation.

Seamanship School

In the winter of 1920–1921 the union conducted a school in seamanship. Besides the evident purpose of developing the skill of the members, there was also the hope that the union school might displace the Sea Service Bureau of the Shipping Board which, of course, turns out non-union seamen. The union school, however, had difficulty in arousing the interest of members. On that account, and because of the strike which followed in May, 1921, the idea has not been revived.

Legislative Policies

The Sailors' Union has persistently sought the aid of legislation to maintain and protect the craft. The provisions of the Seamen's Act which fix a three years' apprenticeship for able seamen (with the exceptions noted in Chapter I), and stipulate that 65 per cent of the deck crew must be able seamen, are obviously intended to maintain seamanship as a skilled craft, and to prevent the displacement of able seamen by ordinaries or landsmen. Legal protection against foreign sailors, particularly Asiatics, is sought in the provision that 75 per cent of the crew of each department must be able to understand any order given by the officers.

These provisions have not proved, in practice, especially helpful to the sailors. The language clause has not prevented the employment of Asiatics who could speak "pidgin English," and in time of strike the issuance of able seamen's certificates has been decidedly liberal.

Of course, these provisions were passed in the name of safety of life and property at sea. The fact that the safety argument is not touched upon here does not mean that it is to be ignored or even discounted. On the contrary, every fresh marine disaster seems to reinforce the contention of those who insist on a high standard of seamanship among the crew.

Freedom and Industrial Democracy

The persistent appeal of the seamen for repeal of laws binding them to involuntary servitude and the tactical importance of that appeal have been discussed in consider-

able detail in earlier chapters.   It remains to note the
broader implications of legal freedom in terms of constitutional government in industry.   While the worker
ashore has been concerning himself with the right of the
group to strike, the sailor has had to start farther back and
against great odds secure the right of the individual to
quit work when the vessel is in safe harbor.   This was a
necessary legal preliminary to the establishment of successful trade unionism among sailors.   The following
quotation indicates that the seamen's leaders are fully conscious of the evolutionary potentialities of the demand
which they have been making.

> Bondmen cannot organize a trade union, because they are not
> in possession of the trade union weapon, namely, the power to
> throw the employer's business out of order by refusing to con-
> tinue labor.   Having obtained this power, the men can then organ-
> ize effectively on trade union lines.   They can, being free men,
> go to the employer and ask for a redress of grievances, and if
> refused they may cease to labor. . . . The employer's business
> usually demands that the work be not too long suspended, and at
> last he listens.   He meets representatives from the men, and
> industrial democracy has begun; it is a fact potentially if not
> practically.   Struggles to come are many and severe before indus-
> try can adjust itself to new conditions; but the beginning is made.

Government Ownership

The seamen, as previously stated, have placed much
reliance on government aid through legislation.   Although
centering their demands on laws which grant new freedom or repeal old restrictions upon it, they have also
worked for laws against advance and allotment, hoping
thus to abolish crimping, for protection of the craft by a
legal minimum standard of skill, for legal protection
against Asiatic seamen, for minimum food, quarters, and
manning standards, and are now seeking to abolish by injunction as an interference with interstate commerce, the
shipowners' employment offices which they have not the

present economic power to abolish themselves. They are also seeking to prohibit by law the grading of men in discharge books in order to protect against possible blacklisting. Anything that smacks of state socialism, however, or even government ownership of the merchant marine, the sailors abhor. As far back as 1894 when the question was agitating the American Federation of Labor, the Sailors' Union went on record against the "collective ownership of the means of production and distribution." And today it opposes government ownership or operation of ships. It takes the view that government ownership of ships means government ownership of the seamen; that the government as shipowner will be its own inspector and supervisor, determining its own safety and manning rules; and that when the seaman strikes he will be striking against the government. The strike of 1921, broken by the United States Shipping Board, demonstrated the helplessness of the men when struggling against the government, and has the more confirmed them in their opposition to government ownership.

Ship Subsidies and Seamen

It is a fact, most frequently observed in the case of the tariff, that workers in an industry commonly support the owners in seeking government aid for that industry. In view of this, the opposition of American seamen to ship subsidies has seemed strange. Although the sailors favor a large American merchant marine, they oppose ship subsidies as a means of building it up, using the arguments generally urged against giving financial aid from the public treasury to any group of citizens. But there seem to be two special reasons which explain the seaman's opposition. In the first place, although the higher American seaman's wage is urged as a reason for the subsidy, the ships on the Pacific which would receive the subsidy carry Oriental and not American seamen. Amendments to subsidy bills providing that no subsidy shall be paid to vessels carrying Chinese crews have been voted down when presented to Congress. Thus American seamen would not be beneficiaries of an act for which their higher wages are prominently held forth as a reason. In the second place, the subsidy proposals, since they are urged largely for nationalistic reasons, usually provide that ships receiving the subsidy shall carry a certain proportion of naval reserve men. This feature is strenuously objected to, because it is regarded as but an entering wedge for the introduction of an *inscripte maritime* like that of France with dangerous strikebreaking possibilities. With such a system, seamen are under naval regulations. Seamen fear that if this is introduced as a voluntary scheme, it is but a step toward making enrolment in the reserve compulsory, and in either case it means the death-blow to the seamen's movement. To train merchant seamen for naval service in time of war, the sailors recommend short enlistment periods of six months, or at most a year, without any following period in the reserve. Nor does a proposal to exclude Chinese seamen from vessels of American registry, providing that the government shall pay the difference between American and Chinese wages, meet with any greater favor. When such a measure was introduced in the House in 1904 the union promptly protested, declaring that such legislation for protecting American seamen should be on the grounds of principle, not of financial profit. The sailors fear that such a scheme would be the means of lowering wages. first on the subsidized ships, then on other vessels.

Shipowners and Seamen

The feeling between shipowners and seamen is not too friendly. For a number of years shipowners have complained, especially on the Pacific coast, of the power of the Sailors' Union. And their opinion of the average sailor is expressed in such terms as "hoodlums," "scum," and "waterfront bums." A writer in the *Pacific Marine Review,* the shipowners' official organ, for December, 1921, described American seamen in these words, referring especially to deep-water sailors, "regrettable as it is to say it, a more despicable, low, drunken, depraved lot of men than the majority of men of the American merchant marine would be hard to find." The sailors for their part believe the owners to be the most "rapacious" and "grasping" of employers, and inefficient in the conduct of the shipping business besides. However, the union policy is to enter into working and wages agreements with the shipowners wherever possible on satisfactory terms.

With few exceptions the policy of the shipowners has been to concede as little as possible in time of prosperity, and to slash wages ruthlessly in times of depression. The shipping business is one of highly fluctuating returns, and the wage policy to which it has naturally led has done nothing to raise the morale of the sailors and build up a satisfied merchant marine personnel.

The union agreements have been made principally with the Shipowners' Association of the Pacific coast. The reason is that the strength of the union membership has always been in the coasting lumber schooners, the owners of which are banded together in that association. With some of the larger steamship lines, informal verbal agreements have been maintained, but none with the

Pacific American Steamship Association, the organization with which most of the large steamship lines are affiliated.

Significance of Lumber Trade to Unionization

The division of economic interest between the owners of the lumber schooners and the owners of the larger steamship lines is one key to the strength of the union on the Pacific coast. The owners of the lumber schooners are generally lumbermen, for whom the interruption of transportation means stoppage of profits on the coastwise lumber trade, instead of merely loss of freights and laying up of ships. This difference of interest among shipowners has manifested itself throughout the history of the union, right down to the present time, and it will probably exist for a long time in the future. It is no mere accident that the men in the lumber schooners have always been the chief strength of the union, that the first agreements were made with the lumber vessel owners back in the sailing ship days, and that in the strike of 1921 the Shipowners' Association of the Pacific coast broke away from the other shipowners to offer separate terms and a higher wage scale.

Trade Agreements

The agreements between union and shipowners have customarily been made for the period of one year, and thereafter until canceled by 30 days' notice in writing. They have provided for the exclusive employment of union crews. The agreement which expired in 1921 was the high-water mark of union achievement in hours and conditions. Wages of able seamen were $90 in all vessels with overtime after eight hours at the rate of 75 cents an hour for ship work, and $1 an hour for working cargo. Through the division of the part of the crew detailed to steer and lookout into three watches, an approximately 8-hour day at sea was also secured. It should be noted here that the union has always recognized the master's sole authority at sea. With the exception of the agreement on three watches, the working regulations apply only in port.

At times, the last occasion being in 1920, the union office has maintained a shipping list, according to which men secured work by turns. Members were given places on the list according to the length of time ashore, the one longest ashore being at the head of the list. Four times a day the list was read, and each man in turn had a chance to accept or reject the jobs offered so long as they lasted. The shipping list caused dissatisfaction among the members because some men let pass many opportunities in order to stand at the head of the list when the best jobs came along, and because others were prevented by the rules of the list from accepting jobs offered them before their turn. The employers preferred greater freedom in the selection of their crews. So after a few months the shipping list was abolished. The owners now ship men through their own employment office, and issue a continuous discharge book in which masters record their opinion of the man's competency which must be presented to secure employment. The union, of course, attacks this as a blacklisting scheme, as they have attacked like plans in the past.

Enforcement of Agreements

Certain difficulties have arisen from time to time in carrying out the agreements. The owners complained of the fact that although the agreement sets a certain wage scale, individual sailors at ports where men were scarce refused to sail at the union rate and demanded higher wages, which the owners were forced to pay. The union did not deny this, but stated that they were unable to compel the men to sail at union rates if they were not individually willing to do so. To exercise compulsion, they said, would result in involuntary servitude. Since the union disciplines men who ship at rates below the union scale, the owners felt, and with some justification, that this position was untenable and that the acts of the union seamen were a violation of the spirit of the agreement.

A further difficulty experienced in carrying out agreements has been the practice sometimes indulged in of signing on, and then backing out at the last moment, thereby perhaps, causing the owner delay and making it difficult to find a crew. By vote of its membership, this conduct has been specifically made an offense against the union, punishable by a fine of not less than $5 for the first offense. For the second, the offender is liable to expulsion.

Not only do individual members make it difficult for the union to carry out its agreements at times, but the branches themselves sometimes defy the authority of headquarters, ignore the union wage scale as fixed by agreement, and strike for higher wages. This difficulty, although it has arisen in the past with branches in the United States, has been confined in recent times chiefly to the branches in British Columbia. The reasons for this independence of the Canadian branches, as stated in Chapter IX, appear to be national prejudice against authority of a headquarters in the United States, differences in ports and territory served, differences in temper of the shore unions with which the branches are affiliated, and differences in ownership of the vessels manned.

Union Strike Policy

The union follows a conservative strike policy, using that weapon only as a last resort. No strike can be declared except by a two-thirds vote of the union, including both headquarters and branches. In case of a possible strike or lockout, no branch can take binding action without the authority of headquarters. In addition to these constitutional precautions of the Sailors' Union, the International Seamen's Union maintains district grievance committees, composed of two representatives from each affiliated union, whose duty it is to adjust grievances between unions and their employers. Although the early history of the Sailors' Union was marked by almost annual strikes, since 1900 (except for the unauthorized action of Canadian branches referred to above) it has engaged in only three strikes, in 1901, 1906, and 1921.

CHAPTER XI

ORGANIZATION AND POLICIES—(Continued)[1]

Relations with Harbor Workers

Contrasting sharply with the cordial relations existing between the various seamen's organizations is the distrust with which the harbor workers are regarded by the Sailors' Union. Throughout the history of the Coast Seamen's and Sailors' Unions, bitter jurisdictional fights have been waged with the longshoremen, particularly on the northwest coast.

The policy of aloofness advocated by Furuseth has been rather consistently followed by the Sailors' Union. The statement given here as the seamen's attitude is therefore based on his official expressions. Individual members, however, and even the union itself, notably in the waterfront strike of 1901 which Furuseth supported, have tried a more conciliatory policy. As described in Chapter IX, a strong group within the union in 1921 threatened to reverse the Furuseth policy. This group was defeated, and many of its members of I. W. W. affiliation expelled. Nevertheless, there is still strong sentiment, particularly among the younger sailors, for closer affiliation with the harbor workers.

Origin of Longshore Work

The underlying condition which has made it necessary that longshoremen work cargo is the increase in size of vessels during recent decades, with a less than proportionate increase in the crew and increased emphasis on

---

[1] Sources for this chapter same as for Chapter X.

quick turn around in port. The seamen, of course, are aware of this fact, but insist on retaining the right of seamen to work cargo, supplemented, if need be, by longshoremen. On the lumber schooners of the Pacific coast this right has been successfully maintained. Elsewhere, and on most classes of vessels, the cargo work has passed into the hands of the longshoremen. The seaman therefore believes that the harbor worker is a usurper of work which was originally his, and which still legally and rightfully belongs to him. The side of the longshoremen coincided with the interest of stevedoring contractors and other shore contractors for work on vessels, who would have less business if the repairing and cargo work were done by sailors. They therefore took the side of the longshoremen and encouraged their encroachment on what was formerly the seamen's work. The seaman's claim to the work of the vessel in the harbor goes back to the days of imprisonment for desertion, when he could be, and was, sent to jail for refusing to do that very work. Indeed, although cargo work has in fact slipped into the hands of the longshoremen almost entirely except on the Pacific coast, both maritime law and custom still require that the sailor shall work cargo when ordered to do so by the master. It is still further loss of cargo work to the longshoremen of which the sailors' leaders are fearful. And to the argument of legal and customary right and law Furuseth adds the argument of advantage to the shipowner and to the nation: Only when the work of keeping the vessel and all her gear in fit condition at all times is given to the seamen will skill in seamanship be developed; the significance of this to the nation is that sea power lies in the skill of the nation's seamen; to the shipowner, a skilled crew means a ship well cared for, well navigated, which can be repaired by her own crew in any port of the world; employment of the crew in discharging and loading means economy because of the high daily wages of the irregularly employed longshoremen, and ensures that men will be present to start loading or discharging immediately upon the arrival of the vessel in port. In the lumber trade, the shipowners have quite consistently supported the seamen against the longshoremen, probably in recognition of the soundness of the economic argument.

Sailors and Marine Federations

Furuseth is distrustful of all federation of shore and marine workers, whether it be a Marine Transportation Department of the American Federation of Labor, which he opposed, or a local waterfront federation. It should be recognized, also, that seamen's leaders have always been active in organizing local and state federations of landworkers. His opposition to federation, it should be noted, is centered on any arrangement which binds the sailors' union to go on strike, except of its own volition. The seamen are included, says Furuseth, for the benefit of the shore workers who saddle the entire burden on the seamen by providing "that no one shall take cargo from or deliver cargo to any non-union man." Since the seaman receives and delivers cargo at the rail it would fall on the seamen to fight for all the federation men on shore. Although in principle the shore workers would fight equally for the seamen, Furuseth's contention is doubtless sound from the standpoint of the seaman's immediate interest at the present time, for the sailors are more strongly organized than the longshoremen. The longshoremen, on the other hand, favor the formation of a federation of transport workers, both local and national, and wish to unite "all watercraft organizations into one big militant body." In fact, the longshoremen are now trying, but with little success, however, to stir up sentiment for a Pacific Coast Federation of Marine Transport Workers (not Marine Transport Workers No. 510 I. W. W.). But Furuseth remembers the long jurisdictional struggle of fifteen years ago over the title, "Longshoremen, Marine and Transport Workers," when the longshoremen claimed jurisdiction over all seamen aboard ship except those of the deck department, the encroachment of longshoremen on cargo work, and their resolutions against the passage of the Seamen's bill; and the protests against the repeal of the Oregon fugitive seamen's law penalizing with three months' imprisonment those who aid a seaman to desert. "With the harbor workers we must insist that they shall quit trying to use us and leave our work alone. On that road and on that road only is friendship and cooperation." Furthermore, he contends that in any affiliation with shore workers, seamen because of their occupation are bound to be in the minority. Not only would this place the sailors' policies in matters of jurisdiction and strikes under the possible domination of others, but it would endanger the realization of freedom for the seamen of all nations by entrusting the program to those not vitally concerned with the seamen's peculiar status under maritime law.

Furuseth and the I. W. W.

As part of the American Federation of Labor, the Sailors' Union is antagonistic to the Industrial Workers of the World, or any similar organization, and to the syndicalistic doctrines of such bodies. As far as concerns the seamen, such an organization has the additional odium, to Furuseth and those who maintain his policies, of another attempt by workers ashore to control the seamen for the shore workers' own ends. Furthermore, the idea of progress by revolution has no part in Furuseth's philosophy. He is skeptical of permanent gains by revolution, and believes democracy in industry will come, if at all, by slow steps, in the same way that democracy has advanced in the religious and political fields. The present conflict of his organization with the Marine Transport Workers, together with a belief that outside influences are now directing I. W. W. policies, has added bitterness to hostility.

Enough has been related of the organization, policies, history, and achievements of the Sailors' Union to make it evident that this is more than an ordinary union. It is distinctive in organization, yet its form of organization is not the foundation of its greatest successes and chief claims to distinction. The foundation is rather the vision and perseverance of its leaders coupled with continuous and loyal support given them by the members of the union.

Seamen's Leaders

Many able leaders have risen from the ranks of the union seamen on the Pacific coast. One of the most prominent of these is Walter Macarthur, now United States Shipping Commissioner in San Francisco. Born on the Clyde in Scotland, he early went to sea before the mast. In the late eighties he came ashore on the Pacific coast, running away from a British ship at San Diego. After a brief period working ashore he reshipped on a coasting vessel. He joined the Coast Seamen's Union, became active in its affairs, and was elected business manager of the *Coast Seamen's Journal*. In the course of time the editor, W. J. B. Mackay, resigned, and Macarthur was put into his place. For practically two decades Macarthur edited the *Journal*, which during his incumbency reached the position of prominence among labor papers which it now occupies. An able speaker, an accurate thinker, and a powerful writer, he used his abilities effectively to advance the cause of the seamen on the coast. In 1913 he resigned from the *Journal* to accept the post of Shipping Commissioner under President Wilson, an office which he has continued to fill under President Harding.

Of the younger seamen, the most prominent is Paul Scharrenberg, a man about forty years of age. He was born in Hamburg, Germany, where he received his early education, and then went to sea. In 1900 or 1901 he came to the Pacific coast as a sailor and joined the union. His ability was noted by older members, and he was put to work as assistant to the business manager of the *Journal*. Later he was made business manager under the editorship of Macarthur. When Macarthur resigned, Scharrenberg was elected to his place. Scharrenberg is a leader of the American Federation of Labor type, thoroughly versed in the phases of the labor movement with which he has to deal, a man of studious inclinations, a good speaker and writer. As editor he maintained the high standard of the *Journal,* and also found time to participate actively in the labor movement of California. For some years he has been Secretary of the State Federation of Labor. In 1921 he was defeated for re-election as editor of the *Journal* by Vance Thompson, as the combined result of a personal feud and a growing revolt against the old leaders and policies. When the International Seamen's Union took over the *Journal* the following year, Scharrenberg was appointed to resume his editorial chair.

Other men of ability have also given much time and effort toward making the seamen's movement a success. There are many of these men who have had visions of better days for the seaman, and who have striven to realize them. Not all who have contributed to the success of the organization were gifted with the qualities which would make them leaders of the union in the office, negotiators with the shipowners, editors of the *Journal,* speakers, or petitioners at the doors of Congress. But a long list might be made of men who built up the union membership in the eighties when organizing seamen was as often a matter of arguing with one's fists as with one's tongue, when no one came to the union office to seek membership, and sailors feared to join because of the warnings of the crimps, when Oriental crews who were carried on the coast could not be kept off except by strong-arm tactics. Loyal and zealous men they were, not afraid of broken heads or days in jail. Little is known of the story of their lives; there is a sameness about them all; they went to sea as boys, sailed for years, finally came to the Pacific coast, deserted or were paid off there, and joined the union. Ed Anderson, now treasurer of the union, was born in Arendal, Norway, in 1857. At the age of 14 he went to sea in a Norwegian brig, sailed several years in the deep-water vessels of nine different nations, came to the Pacific in 1877, again in 1878, and finally in 1881. There he worked at various occupations ashore and at intervals went to sea in coasting vessels. Throughout the early years of the union he served as patrolman on the waterfront. Tom Finnerty, of Irish descent, came to the coast in 1886, deserting a British ship from Australia. John Murray, an Englishman, deserted from a British ship in 1883 and when the union was organized patrolled the waterfront with Andersen and the rest. Jim Leighton, an Englishman, long agent of the union in San Pedro, Jim McCleran, an Irishman who came to the coast in 1887, Peter B. Gill, a Norwegian who came to the coast in 1885 or 1886, now agent in Seattle, and Oscar Baldwin, a Swede who was paid off from an American vessel on the coast in 1886 or 1887, and was agent of the union at Eureka, were all leading members of this group. John P. Hansen, a Norwegian who came to the coast in 1885, now a retired sea captain, Alfred Fuhrman, a German sailor, later leader of the brewery workers, and Andrew Olesen, a Norwegian sailor who' came to the coast in 1886, were also among the men who made possible the continued existence of the union in the precarious period of its early existence. These are only a few of those that deserve mention and are typical of many who have contributed from 1885 down to the present time to the organized seamen's movement on the Pacific coast.

Of the seamen who have persevered and sacrificed for the men of their calling, none has persevered more, sacrificed more, accomplished more for seamen than Andrew Furuseth. Furuseth was born at Romedal, Hedemarken, in Norway, in 1854, and like other boys of the time went to sea early in a Norwegian deep-water square-rigger. For ten or twelve years he sailed, working in vessels of seven different nations. In 1880 he came to the Pacific coast in an English ship from Calcutta, left her here, and went fishing on the Columbia River. When the sailors of San Francisco met on the lumber pile on Folsom Street wharf in March, 1885, to form a union, Furuseth was away fishing, but upon his return a few months later he allied himself with the organization. The following year he was elected secretary, but as he was unwilling at the time to serve, John Haist was chosen in his place. In 1887, however, Furuseth was again elected, and this time took office. Since that time he has served the union as secretary practically continuously. In March, 1892, he suddenly resigned and again joined the fishermen, giving as his reason that many members thought he had "grown fast in his seat." A substitute was put in office, but with the approach of the impending struggle with the ship-owners, the first skirmishes of which occurred in May and June, appeals were sent to Furuseth to return. On May 30, 1892, he finally agreed to come back and resume the duties of secretary. Much of his life since 1894 has been spent in Washington in the interest of seamen's legislation and as president of the International Seamen's Union. It has therefore become customary in the Sailors' Union to elect Furuseth as secretary, and to choose the man who serves actively as secretary pro tem.

Andrew Furuseth is a tall, bony figure, stoop-should-ered, always clad in a dark coat and creaseless trousers which hang about his legs in folds. The profile of his Norse face stands out "like the prow of a Viking ship," and there is an agressive set to his chin and slightly pro-truding underlip. His strong face is deeply furrowed, his eyes are keen and penetrating, and his voice high-pitched and piercing. Still vigorous in spite of his 69 years, he gives the impression of tremendous aggressive power, of a man forceful and tireless.

From the day when he first fully realized the social and economic significance to the sailor of his peculiar legal status, he has devoted his life unreservedly to the cause of abolishing involuntary servitude among seamen, first among seamen of the United States, and then of the world. He has mastered the provisions of the ancient maritime laws relating to seamen, and has studied the navigation laws of modern nations so as to be able the more con-vincingly to present the cause of the seaman. For the same reason he has studied the best models of English style, so that in writing or speaking his arguments and appeals may be more effective. The result is that his appeals and exhortations, both written and oral, ring like trumpet calls and that in spite of a certain carelessness of the rules of grammar his writings exhibit an enviable purity of style. The richness of his imagery, his frequent and original illustrations, the evident sincerity and idealism of the man, all combine to give to his expressions a rare clearness, vividness, and power.

Shipowners and labor leaders who oppose him regard him as a crank, a fanatic. Others think him just queer. His ardent followers sometimes call him the "Abraham Lincoln of the Sea." None has ever questioned the wholeheartedness of his devotion to the cause of the seamen, or his personal disinterestedness. Owners who have had dealings with Furuseth for many years aver that he is personally incorruptible. Opponents within the labor movement, both in and out of his union, accuse him of riding roughshod over opposition, but they, like the shipowners, agree that his motives are without the slightest taint of suspicion. He himself never has taken more salary than was necessary to keep body and soul together in health and vigor, to buy books (for he is a great reader), and supply his pipe with tobacco. Although he has repeatedly been sent on missions to Europe as representative of the seamen and even of the government, and has frequented the halls and committee rooms of Congress for over a quarter of a century, his habits of life have remained frugal. He has never married, and his only home in San Francisco is a room not a great deal larger than a sailor's space in a forecastle. In Washington, he lived first in the Keystone Hotel, then in the old National Hotel on Pennsylvania Avenue. Persons living in the neighborhood used to complain to the hotel of someone who disturbed their sleep by pounding on a typewriter until three or four in the morning.

A strong strain of melancholy, characteristic of Norse peoples, runs through Furuseth's makeup. His achievements have been as often followed by depression as by exaltation. Many times he has closed up his desk and left the union office at night saying to himself that he would never return. But early the next morning he always came back. He does not confide even in his closest friends. Men who have known him longest preface their answers to questions about his personal history with "Well, nobody knows much about him." Fremont Older tells one of the best known stories. A good many years ago Furuseth was defendant in court proceedings growing out of an injunction. When Older spoke of the possibility of a jail sentence, Furuseth replied slowly and with measured emphasis, "They can't put me in a smaller room than I've always lived in, they can't give me plainer food than I've always eaten, they can't make me any lonelier than I've always been."

Courageous, sincere, devoted to his ideals, possessed of great spiritual power, this is the man who in 1915 brought freedom to the seamen of the United States, and who in 1920 secured the adoption of his program of freedom by the seamen of the world. He is a strong individualist, who believes that men, or groups of men, must maintain themselves by their own efforts or go down to deserved defeat. He works for the seamen, and the seamen alone. He plays a lone hand, and cares little for the support of other groups of workers except as they aid the preservation or enforcement of the Seamen's Act. Of the longshoremen he asks only that they leave the seamen alone. The motto which he coined for the union fits the man: "Never beg bread from friend, nor mercy from enemy, live by your own strength or die." He is often defeated, and acknowledges it, but he never is beaten. From the days of the crushing defeat of 1893 down to the present he has reiterated his other motto after every reverse or disappointment: "Tomorrow is also a day."

With Furuseth the emancipation of the seaman is not solely a means of bettering the seaman's economic position, although it includes that. It is also a means of improving his social position, of giving him self-respect, and entitling him to the respect of others, of restoring him to an honorable calling with the same rights and privileges possessed by free workers ashore. In 1897, just after the decision of the Supreme Court in the Arago case, holding that the thirteenth amendment abolishing involuntary servitude did not apply to seamen, Furuseth replied in these words to the invitation to participate in the San Francisco Independence Day parade:

> We, therefore, sir, being mindful of our status—that of involuntary servitude—which was in no way modified by that declaration of individual freedom, feel that it would be an imposition on our part to take advantage of your kindness and inflict our presence—the presence of bondmen—upon the freemen who will on the Fourth of July celebrate their freedom and renew their allegiance to those principles which have made nations and men great. Hoping that we also some day may honorably and as equals march in such parade, we are faithfully yours,
>
> THE SAILORS' UNION,
> per A. FURUSETH, *Secretary.*

In 1909, the following appeal, penned by Furuseth, was adopted by the International Seamen's Union of America, and in the following year by the International Transport Workers' Congress at Copenhagen:

> To those who govern nations, to those who make the laws, to humanitarians, democrats, Christians, and friends of human freedom everywhere, do we, the seamen, the yet remaining bondmen, humbly yet earnestly submit this our petition, that we be made free men, and that the blighting disgrace of bondage be removed from our labor, which once was considered honorable, which is yet needed in the world of commerce, and which has been held to be of great importance to nations with seacoasts to defend.
>
> Existing maritime law makes of seamen, excepting in the

domestic trade of the United States, the property of the vessel on which we sail. We cannot work as seamen without signing a contract which brings us under the law. This contract is fixed by law or authorized by governments. We have nothing to do with its terms. We either sign it and sail, or we sign it not and remain landsmen.

When signing this contract, we surrender our working power to the will of another man at all times until the contract expires. We may not, on pain of penal punishment, fail to join the vessel. We may not leave the vessel, though she is in perfect safety. We may not, without our master's permission, go to a mother's sick bed or funeral, or attend to any other duties of a son, a brother, a Christian, or a citizen, excepting in the domestic trade of the United States.

If the owner thinks he has reason to fear that we desire to escape, he may, without judicial investigation, cause us to be imprisoned for safe-keeping until he shall think proper to take us out. If we have escaped, he may publish our personal appearance along with a reward for our apprehension and return. He may, through contracts between nations, cause the peace officers and police to aid him in recovering his property. The Captain may change, the owner may change—we are sold with the vessel—but so long as the flag does not change, there is nothing except serious illness or our master's pleasure that will release us from the vessel.

The master, acting for the vessel, may release himself and the vessel by paying a few dollars, with no alternative.

He that owns another man's labor power owns his body, since the two cannot be separated.

.   .   .   .   .

We now raise our manacled hands in humble supplication and pray that the nations issue a decree of emancipation and restore to us our right as brother men; to our labor that honor which belonged to it until your power, expressing itself through your law, set upon it the brand of bondage in the interest of cheap transportation by water.

.   .   .   .   .

We further submit that, as the consciousness of the seaman's status penetrates through the population, it will be impossible to get freemen to send their sons into bondage or to induce freemen's sons to accept it, and we, in all candor, remind you that you, when you travel by water, expect us—the serfs—to exhibit in danger the highest qualities of freemen by giving our lives for your safety.

At sea the law of common hazard remains. There must be discipline and self-sacrifice, but in any harbor the vessel and you are safe, and we beseech you to give us that freedom which you claim for yourself and which you have bestowed on others, to the end that we may be relieved of that bitterness of soul that is the heavy burden of him who knows and feels that his body is not his own.

While Furuseth was still fighting for the abolition of imprisonment for desertion in the United States, he carried his program to the seamen of other nations, a program which they have not received with open arms. Their attention had been centered principally on the passage of remedial legislation, such as old-age pensions, pensions to widows and orphans, accident compensation, medical treatment, regulation of Sunday labor, pay for overtime work, etc. The American program on the contrary sought first the release of the economic power of seamen. As stated by Andrew Furuseth:

> In Europe the seamen are looking for more laws, which mean less freedom, while we here have been engaged in having laws repealed, and seeking to enact [the type of] laws that will guard and increase personal freedom. Our success, which is greater than theirs, rests upon this foundation . . . . and if the seamen of Europe can be made to understand the importance of changing their policy, so that they will demand from the people on shore equal rights with them, and as a preliminary thereto, demand absolute and indisputable ownership in their own bodies, then time and money will be well expended.

The British seamen, from the time when the Coast Seamen's Union first sent delegates to their Glasgow convention to the present time, have not been in entire sympathy with his proposals, and have not regarded the right to quit the ship in safe harbors as paramount. Indeed, they have said that they did not want their men to desert in foreign ports, but thought it better for them, financially and otherwise, to stay by their vessels and return with them to the British Isles. Likewise, they feared that allowing foreign seamen to desert in the British Isles would make it too easy to bring in strikebreaking seamen from the Continental countries close by and that a relaxation of the bonds between seamen and the vessel might facilitate the substitution of Lascars for British east of Suez.

In 1908, Furuseth again took his proposals to Europe. At that time there was no federation of seafarers, so that the only way by which Furuseth could lay his program before the seamen of Europe in Convention was by presenting it at the Vienna Congress of the International Transport Workers' Congress, which included seamen and harbor workers. He presented his program; but the European delegates, many of whom were socialists, pronounced him a visionary, a dreamer. Paul Muller, the German delegate, declared his legislative proposals so preposterous and indeed "anarchistic" that no one would dare to take them into the Reichstag, and led the opposition which prevented action on the American proposal. Two years later (1910), however, the American petition quoted above was adopted by the Copenhagen Congress of the International Transport Workers' Federation.

Years passed by, and the seamen of the world had formed their own International Seafarers' Federation. This separation from the Transport Workers was opposed by some of the leaders in the latter organization, whereupon the International Seamen's Union of America withdrew from the Transport Federation, in conformity with its traditional policy of isolation.

In 1920, Furuseth and the American delegation again carried their proposals embodying the principles of the Seamen's Act to Europe, this time for adoption by the seamen of the world meeting in their own federation. The first, or "Open Conference" at Genoa was held as a preliminary to the League of Nations International Labor Conference. Seamen of all grades including officers were admitted, and delegates' votes were not weighted according to number of seamen represented. At this conference the American resolutions demanding abolition of imprisonment for desertion were defeated.

Next followed the International Labor Conference to consider problems of seamen, under the auspices of the League of Nations, also held at Genoa. Each country was represented by four delegates, two appointed by the government, one by the shipowners, and one by the seamen. This conference endorsed principles favoring the abolition of criminal penalties for breach of the seamen's contract, but with this limitation: Although shipowners, according to the resolution passed, were denied the right to invoke these penalties against the seamen, the public authorities were allowed to enforce them in cases of "violations of the clauses [of the contract] of a public character, maintaining public policy as distinguished from private interests."

World's Seamen Endorse American Policies

Two months later the International Seafarers' Federation held their own Congress at Brussels. The American delegates, Andrew Furuseth, Oscar Carlson, and Paul Scharrenberg again put forth their program demanding the right to quit the vessel in safe harbors, and the abolition of criminal penalties for breach of the seamen's contract of personal service. This program was adopted without a dissenting vote, the seamen of the world thus placing themselves on record as endorsing the basic policies for which Furuseth, backed by the rank and file of his union, had fought for more than thirty years.

The goal of Andrew Furuseth and the seamen of America still lies ahead. Freedom to quit the vessel in safe harbor has been won in ports of the United States. The seamen of the world in convention, have endorsed the demand for freedom. But Furuseth will not rest until the laws of all nations give seamen equal rights with workers ashore. Writing during the war, he said:

It is true that the seamen of Great Britain, as well as of other countries, are yet bondmen. It may also be true that when this world war is over, the joy in its ending may again cause the people to forget; but we shall not permit the people to forget. We seamen shall remind them again and again until the present expressions of appreciation and resolutions of thanks shall be translated into statutes, which will in all countries make the seamen free and shall give to us seamen the opportunity to reconquer our true place among men.

No matter what happens, we may expect to see Andrew Furuseth fighting to his dying day for the freedom of those who go down to the sea in ships.

INDEX

American Labor: From Conspiracy to Collective Bargaining

AN ARNO PRESS/NEW YORK TIMES COLLECTION

SERIES I

Abbott, Edith.
Women in Industry. 1913.

Aveling, Edward B. and Eleanor M. Aveling.
Working Class Movement in America. 1891.

Beard, Mary.
The American Labor Movement. 1939.

Blankenhorn, Heber.
The Strike for Union. 1924.

Blum, Solomon.
Labor Economics. 1925.

Brandeis, Louis D. and Josephine Goldmark.
Women in Industry. 1907. New introduction by Leon Stein and
    Philip Taft.

Brooks, John Graham.
American Syndicalism. 1913.

Butler, Elizabeth Beardsley.
Women and the Trades. 1909.

Byington, Margaret Frances.
Homestead: The Household of A Mill Town. 1910.

Carroll, Mollie Ray.
Labor and Politics. 1923.

Coleman, McAlister.
Men and Coal. 1943.

Coleman, J. Walter.
The Molly Maguire Riots: Industrial Conflict in the Pennsylvania Coal Region. 1936.

Commons, John R.
Industrial Goodwill. 1919.

Commons, John R.
Industrial Government. 1921.

Dacus, Joseph A.
Annals of the Great Strikes. 1877.

Dealtry, William.
The Laborer: A Remedy for his Wrongs. 1869.

Douglas, Paul H., Curtis N. Hitchcock and Willard E. Atkins, editors.
The Worker in Modern Economic Society. 1923.

Eastman, Crystal.
Work Accidents and the Law. 1910.

Ely, Richard T.
The Labor Movement in America. 1890. New Introduction by Leon Stein and Philip Taft.

Feldman, Herman.
Problems in Labor Relations. 1937.

Fitch, John Andrew.
The Steel Worker. 1910.

Furniss, Edgar S. and Laurence Guild.
Labor Problems. 1925.

Gladden, Washington.
Working People and Their Employers. 1885.

Gompers, Samuel.
Labor and the Common Welfare. 1919.

Hardman, J. B. S., editor.
American Labor Dynamics. 1928.

Higgins, George G.
Voluntarism in Organized Labor, 1930-40. 1944.

Hiller, Ernest T.
The Strike. 1928.

Hollander, Jacob S. and George E. Barnett.
Studies in American Trade Unionism. 1906. New Introduction by
Leon Stein and Philip Taft.

Jelley, Symmes M.
The Voice of Labor. 1888.

Jones, Mary.
Autobiography of Mother Jones. 1925.

Kelley, Florence.
Some Ethical Gains Through Legislation. 1905.

LaFollette, Robert M., editor.
The Making of America: Labor. 1906.

Lane, Winthrop D.
Civil War in West Virginia. 1921.

Lauck, W. Jett and Edgar Sydenstricker.
Conditions of Labor in American Industries. 1917.

Leiserson, William M.
Adjusting Immigrant and Industry. 1924.

Lescohier, Don D.
Knights of St. Crispin. 1910.

Levinson, Edward.
I Break Strikes. The Technique of Pearl L. Bergoff. 1935.

Lloyd, Henry Demarest.
Men, The Workers. Compiled by Anne Whithington and
Caroline Stallbohen. 1909. New Introduction by Leon Stein
and Philip Taft.

Lorwin, Louis (Louis Levine).
The Women's Garment Workers. 1924.

Markham, Edwin, Ben B. Lindsay and George Creel.
Children in Bondage. 1914.

Marot, Helen.
American Labor Unions. 1914.

Mason, Alpheus T.
Organized Labor and the Law. 1925.

Newcomb, Simon.
A Plain Man's Talk on the Labor Question. 1886. New Introduction
by Leon Stein and Philip Taft.

Price, George Moses.
The Modern Factory: Safety, Sanitation and Welfare. 1914.

Randall, John Herman Jr.
Problem of Group Responsibility to Society. 1922.

Rubinow, I. M.
Social Insurance. 1913.

Saposs, David, editor.
Readings in Trade Unionism. 1926.

Slichter, Sumner H.
Union Policies and Industrial Management. 1941.

Socialist Publishing Society.
The Accused and the Accusers. 1887.

Stein, Leon and Philip Taft, editors.
The Pullman Strike. 1894-1913. New Introduction by the editors.

Stein, Leon and Philip Taft, editors.
Religion, Reform, and Revolution: Labor Panaceas in the Nineteenth
Century. 1969. New Introduction by the editors.

Stein, Leon and Philip Taft, editors.
Wages, Hours, and Strikes: Labor Panaceas in the Twentieth Century.
1969. New introduction by the editors.

Swinton, John.
A Momentous Question: The Respective Attitudes of Labor and Capital. 1895. New Introduction by Leon Stein and Philip Taft.

Tannenbaum, Frank.
The Labor Movement. 1921.

Tead, Ordway.
Instincts in Industry. 1918.

Vorse, Mary Heaton.
Labor's New Millions. 1938.

Witte, Edwin Emil.
The Government in Labor Disputes. 1932.

Wright, Carroll D.
The Working Girls of Boston. 1889.

Wyckoff, Veitrees J.
Wage Policies of Labor Organizations in a Period of Industrial Depression. 1926.

Yellen, Samuel.
American Labor Struggles. 1936.

SERIES II

Allen, Henry J.
The Party of the Third Part: The Story of the Kansas Industrial Relations Court. 1921. *Including* **The Kansas Court of Industrial Relations Law** (1920) by Samuel Gompers.

Baker, Ray Stannard.
The New Industrial Unrest. 1920.

Barnett, George E. & David A. McCabe.
Mediation, Investigation and Arbitration in Industrial Disputes. 1916.

Barns, William E., editor.
The Labor Problem. 1886.

Bing, Alexander M.
War-Time Strikes and Their Adjustment. 1921.

Brooks, Robert R. R.
When Labor Organizes. 1937.

Calkins, Clinch.
Spy Overhead: The Story of Industrial Espionage. 1937.

Cooke, Morris Llewellyn & Philip Murray.
Organized Labor and Production. 1940.

Creamer, Daniel & Charles W. Coulter.
Labor and the Shut-Down of the Amoskeag Textile Mills. 1939.

Glocker, Theodore W.
The Government of American Trade Unions. 1913.

Gompers, Samuel.
Labor and the Employer. 1920.

Grant, Luke.
The National Erectors' Association and the International Association of Bridge and Structural Ironworkers. 1915.

Haber, William.
Industrial Relations in the Building Industry. 1930.

Henry, Alice.
Women and the Labor Movement. 1923.

Herbst, Alma.
The Negro in the Slaughtering and Meat-Packing Industry in Chicago. 1932.

[Hicks, Obediah.]
Life of Richard F. Trevellick. 1896.

Hillquit, Morris, Samuel Gompers & Max J. Hayes.
The Double Edge of Labor's Sword: Discussion and Testimony on Socialism and Trade-Unionism Before the Commission on Industrial Relations. 1914. New Introduction by Leon Stein and Philip Taft.

Jensen, Vernon H.
Lumber and Labor. 1945.

Kampelman, Max M.
The Communist Party vs. the C.I.O. 1957.

Kingsbury, Susan M., editor.
Labor Laws and Their Enforcement. By Charles E. Persons, Mabel Parton, Mabelle Moses & Three "Fellows." 1911.

McCabe, David A.
The Standard Rate in American Trade Unions. 1912.

Mangold, George Benjamin.
Labor Argument in the American Protective Tariff Discussion. 1908.

Millis, Harry A., editor.
How Collective Bargaining Works. 1942.

Montgomery, Royal E.
Industrial Relations in the Chicago Building Trades. 1927.

Oneal, James.
The Workers in American History. 3rd edition, 1912.

Palmer, Gladys L.
Union Tactics and Economic Change: A Case Study of Three Philadelphia Textile Unions. 1932.

Penny, Virginia.
How Women Can Make Money: Married or Single, In all Branches of the Arts and Sciences, Professions, Trades, Agricultural and Mechanical Pursuits. 1870. New Introduction by Leon Stein and Philip Taft.

Penny, Virginia.
Think and Act: A Series of Articles Pertaining to Men and Women, Work and Wages. 1869.

Pickering, John.
The Working Man's Political Economy. 1847.

Ryan, John A.
A Living Wage. 1906.

Savage, Marion Dutton.
Industrial Unionism in America. 1922.

Simkhovitch, Mary Kingsbury.
The City Worker's World in America. 1917.

Spero, Sterling Denhard.
The Labor Movement in a Government Industry: A Study of Employee Organization in the Postal Service. 1927.

Stein, Leon and Philip Taft, editors.
Labor Politics: Collected Pamphlets. 2 vols. 1836-1932. New Introduction by the editors.

Stein, Leon and Philip Taft, editors.
The Management of Workers: Selected Arguments. 1917-1956. New Introduction by the editors.

Stein, Leon and Philip Taft, editors.
Massacre at Ludlow: Four Reports. 1914-1915. New Introduction by the editors.

Stein, Leon and Philip Taft, editors.
Workers Speak: Self-Portraits. 1902-1906. New Introduction by the editors.

Stolberg, Benjamin.
The Story of the CIO. 1938.

Taylor, Paul S.
The Sailors' Union of the Pacific. 1923.

U.S. Commission on Industrial Relations.
Efficiency Systems and Labor. 1916. New Introduction by Leon Stein and Philip Taft.

Walker, Charles Rumford.
American City: A Rank-and-File History. 1937.

Walling, William English.
American Labor and American Democracy. 1926.

Williams, Whiting.
What's on the Worker's Mind: By One Who Put on Overalls to Find Out. 1920.

Wolman, Leo.
The Boycott in American Trade Unions. 1916.

Ziskind, David.
One Thousand Strikes of Government Employees. 1940.